Thriving in Turbulent Times:
Strategies for Resilience and Renewal:

Navigating Uncertainty with Grace, Courage, and Inner Strength

BY
ADEEL ANJUM

CONTENTS

INTRODUCTION   1

Chapter 01
Embracing Turbulence 4

Strategies for Resilience

Chapter 02
Cultivating Emotional Resilience 11
Chapter 03
Nurturing Physical Resilience 17
Chapter 04
Strengthening Mental Resilience 22
Chapter 05
Fostering Social Resilience 27

Strategies for Renewal

Chapter 06
Finding Balance in Chaos 34
Chapter 07
Embracing Change 39
Chapter 08
Cultivating Gratitude 45
Chapter 09
Harnessing Creativity 51

Integrating Resilience and Renewal

Chapter 10
Building Resilient Habits 58

Chapter 11
Mindfulness in Action 68
Chapter 12
Building Inner Strength 74
Chapter 13
Navigating Uncertainty 80
Chapter 14
Adaptive Leadership 87
Chapter 15
Resilient Communication 93
Chapter 16
Finding Meaning in Adversity 98
Chapter 17
Resilient Decision Making 104
Chapter 18
Adaptive Problem-Solving 110
Chapter 19
Resilient Relationships 116
Chapter 20
Celebrating Resilience 122
Chapter 21
Cultivating Resilient Mindsets 128
Chapter 22
Building Resilient Communities 134
Chapter 23
Sustaining Resilient Practices 140
Chapter 24
Resilience in Times of Crisis 146
Chapter 25
Legacy of Resilience 152

CONCLUSION   **158**

INTRODUCTION

In the turbulent seas of life, amidst the crashing waves of uncertainty and adversity, there exists a beacon of light – resilience. Resilience, the ability to bounce back from setbacks, adapt to change, and thrive in the face of challenges, is a fundamental human trait that has enabled individuals and societies to endure and overcome even the most daunting of obstacles throughout history. It is the force that propels us forward, empowering us to transform adversity into opportunity, chaos into clarity, and despair into hope.

Welcome to "Thriving in Turbulent Times: Strategies for Resilience and Renewal." In this book, we embark on a journey of exploration and discovery, delving into the depths of resilience and renewal to uncover the strategies, insights, and wisdom that can empower us to navigate life's challenges with courage, grace, and resilience.

Our journey begins with an exploration of the nature of turbulence in Chapter 1, where we learn to embrace uncertainty as a catalyst for change and growth. From there, we delve into the core pillars of resilience – emotional, physical, mental, and social – in Chapters 2 through 5, uncovering the practices and principles that enable us to cultivate strength and fortitude in every aspect of our lives.

As we journey further, we explore the strategies for renewal in Chapters 6 through 9, discovering how to find balance in chaos, harness creativity, and cultivate gratitude as pathways to inner peace and fulfillment. We then turn our gaze to the integration of resilience and renewal in Chapters 10 through 13, where we learn to build resilient habits, embrace mindfulness, and cultivate inner strength as the foundation for a resilient life.

In the final chapters of our journey, we explore the broader implications of resilience in Chapters 14 through 17, examining its role in leadership, communication, decision-making, and problem-solving. We also reflect on the legacy of resilience in Chapters 18 through 21, celebrating the resilience of our ancestors, passing down resilience skills to future generations, and inspiring hope and courage for a resilient future.

Throughout this book, we will draw upon the wisdom of philosophers, poets, leaders, and everyday heroes to illuminate the path ahead. We will share stories of triumph over adversity, practical strategies for building resilience, and timeless principles for navigating life's challenges with grace and resilience. Together, we will embark on a journey of transformation and renewal, uncovering the resilience within us and empowering ourselves to thrive in the midst of turbulence.

So, join me as we embark on this journey of exploration and discovery, as we uncover the secrets of resilience and renewal, and as we learn to thrive in turbulent times with grace, courage, and inner strength. The journey ahead may be challenging, but with resilience as our guide, there is no limit to what we can achieve.

Chapter 01

Embracing Turbulence

"In the midst of chaos, there is also opportunity." - Sun Tzu

Navigating the stormy seas of life can be daunting. We're often taught to seek stability, to crave predictability, and to shy away from chaos. Yet, hidden within the turbulence lies a profound opportunity for growth and transformation. In this chapter, we will delve into the heart of turbulence, exploring its nature, uncovering its hidden potentials, and learning how to embrace it as a catalyst for personal and professional development.

Understanding the Nature of Turbulence

Turbulence is inherent in the fabric of existence. It manifests in various forms – from sudden upheavals in our personal lives to seismic shifts in the global landscape. Whether it's the unexpected loss of a job, a health crisis, or a socio-political upheaval, turbulence disrupts the equilibrium of our lives, challenging our sense of stability and security.

At its core, turbulence is characterized by unpredictability, volatility, and complexity. It's the moment when the familiar ground beneath our feet starts to quake, leaving us feeling disoriented and vulnerable. However, amidst the chaos, there's an underlying order – a hidden pattern waiting to be deciphered. Understanding this nature of turbulence is the first step toward navigating it effectively.

Turbulence often emerges unexpectedly, catching us off guard and testing our resilience. It can be triggered by external factors such as economic downturns, natural disasters, or political unrest, or it can arise from internal sources such as personal crises, relationship challenges, or existential questioning. Regardless of its origins, turbulence disrupts our sense of stability and forces us to confront the uncomfortable reality of impermanence.

Recognizing the Potential for Growth within Chaos

While turbulence may evoke fear and anxiety, it also carries within it the seeds of opportunity. Just as a forest fire clears the way for new growth, turbulent times can pave the path for personal and collective renewal. It's during these tumultuous periods that we're pushed beyond our comfort zones, forced to confront our limitations, and compelled to innovate and adapt.

History is replete with examples of individuals and societies that have thrived in the face of adversity. From the Renaissance that emerged from the ashes of the Black Death to the technological revolution spurred by economic downturns, turbulence has often been the breeding ground for creativity, resilience, and progress. By reframing our perspective, we can begin to see turbulence not as a threat but as an opportunity for growth and renewal.

Within every challenge lies an opportunity for learning and growth. Turbulent times force us to question our assumptions, rethink our priorities, and reimagine our possibilities. They invite us to step outside our comfort zones, explore new territories, and discover untapped reservoirs of strength and resilience within ourselves. By embracing the discomfort of uncertainty and leaning into the challenges that arise, we can harness the transformative power of turbulence to propel us toward our highest potential.

Embracing Uncertainty as a Catalyst for Change

Uncertainty is the hallmark of turbulent times. It's the feeling of stepping into the unknown, with no clear path ahead. Yet, it's precisely this uncertainty that can ignite the fires of transformation. When the ground beneath us shifts, it compels us to question our assumptions, to challenge the status quo, and to explore new possibilities.

Embracing uncertainty doesn't mean succumbing to fear or paralysis. Instead, it's about cultivating a sense of curiosity and adventure – a willingness to venture into the unknown and discover what lies beyond the horizon. It's about embracing the journey rather than fixating on the destination, trusting in our ability to navigate the twists and turns along the way.

In uncertain times, we're forced to relinquish our attachment to control and embrace the fluidity of life. We learn to adapt to changing circumstances, to pivot when necessary, and to find strength in the midst of uncertainty. Rather than viewing uncertainty as a threat, we can choose to see it as an invitation to explore new possibilities, to innovate, and to grow. By embracing uncertainty as a catalyst for change, we can harness its transformative power to shape our lives in meaningful and unexpected ways.

Cultivating a Mindset of Adaptability and Resilience

In the face of turbulence, adaptability and resilience become invaluable assets. Rather than clinging to rigid structures or predefined plans, we must learn to bend with the wind, to pivot when necessary, and to bounce back from setbacks stronger than before. Cultivating these qualities requires a shift in mindset – from one of rigidity to one of flexibility, from one of victimhood to one of empowerment.

Adaptability is about staying nimble and responsive in the face of change, embracing experimentation and iteration as we chart our course forward. Resilience, on the other hand, is about bouncing back from adversity, learning from failure, and harnessing our inner strength to persevere in the face of challenges.

In essence, embracing turbulence is not about seeking refuge from the storm but learning to dance in the rain. It's about finding beauty amidst the chaos, strength amidst the struggle, and opportunity amidst the uncertainty. By understanding the nature of turbulence, recognizing its potential for growth, embracing uncertainty as a catalyst for change, and cultivating a mindset of adaptability and resilience, we can not only survive but thrive in turbulent times.

Adaptability is a skill that can be honed through practice and self-awareness. It involves staying open to new ideas, being willing to experiment, and embracing failure as a natural part of the learning process. By cultivating a growth mindset, we can approach challenges with curiosity and optimism, seeing them as opportunities for growth rather than obstacles to be avoided.

Resilience, likewise, can be cultivated through intentional effort and practice. It involves developing coping mechanisms, building a strong support network, and cultivating a sense of self-efficacy. By reframing setbacks as temporary setbacks rather than insurmountable obstacles, we can bounce back from adversity with renewed determination and resilience.

In summary, embracing turbulence requires a shift in mindset – from one of fear and resistance to one of curiosity and resilience. By understanding the nature of turbulence, recognizing its potential for growth, embracing uncertainty as a catalyst for change, and cultivating a mindset of adaptability and resilience, we can not only survive but thrive in turbulent times. As we embark on this journey of self-discovery and transformation, let us remember the words of Sun Tzu: "In the midst of chaos, there is also opportunity."

Strategies for Resilience

Chapter 02

Cultivating Emotional Resilience

"The only way out is through." - Robert Frost

Emotional resilience is the bedrock upon which our ability to navigate turbulent times rests. In the face of adversity, it's our capacity to understand, manage, and bounce back from our emotions that determines our resilience. In this chapter, we will explore the strategies for cultivating emotional resilience, drawing on wisdom from psychology, neuroscience, and personal development.

Developing Emotional Awareness and Regulation

The first step toward cultivating emotional resilience is developing awareness of our emotional landscape. Often, we're so caught up in the whirlwind of our thoughts and feelings that we lose sight of their underlying causes and triggers. By practicing mindfulness and self-reflection, we can learn to observe our emotions without judgment, gaining insight into their origins and patterns.

Emotional awareness involves recognizing the full spectrum of our emotions – from joy and gratitude to anger and sadness – and acknowledging them without resistance or suppression. It's about creating space for our emotions to be felt and expressed, rather than pushing them away or denying their existence. Through mindfulness practices such as meditation, journaling, and body scan exercises, we can cultivate a deeper connection to our emotional experiences, allowing us to navigate them with greater ease and clarity.

Emotional regulation is the ability to manage our emotions in healthy and adaptive ways. It involves recognizing when our emotions are escalating and taking proactive steps to soothe ourselves. Techniques such as deep breathing, progressive muscle relaxation, and cognitive reframing can help us regain control over our emotional responses, allowing us to respond to challenges with greater calm and clarity.

Moreover, emotional regulation entails understanding the triggers and patterns that contribute to our emotional states. By identifying our personal triggers – whether they're certain situations, people, or thoughts – we can develop strategies to minimize their impact and cultivate greater emotional stability. For example, if public speaking induces anxiety, we might practice relaxation techniques beforehand or challenge negative thoughts about our performance.

Practicing Self-Compassion and Acceptance

Self-compassion is the antidote to self-criticism and harsh judgment. It involves treating ourselves with kindness and understanding, especially in times of difficulty. Rather than berating ourselves for our perceived shortcomings or failures, we can learn to embrace ourselves with warmth and acceptance, recognizing that we're doing the best we can with the resources we have.

Self-compassion involves three core components: self-kindness, common humanity, and mindfulness. Self-kindness entails extending the same care and compassion to ourselves that we would to a close friend in need. It's about offering ourselves words of encouragement, comfort, and support, especially when we're facing challenges or setbacks.

Common humanity involves recognizing that suffering is a universal human experience – something that we all encounter at various points in our lives. Rather than feeling isolated or ashamed of our struggles, we can find solace in the knowledge that we're not alone in our suffering. This sense of connection to others can provide us with a source of comfort and validation, helping us to navigate difficult times with greater resilience and grace.

Mindfulness is the practice of being present and aware of our thoughts, feelings, and sensations without judgment. By cultivating mindfulness, we can observe our inner experiences with curiosity and compassion, rather than getting caught up in them or trying to push them away. This nonjudgmental awareness allows us to create space for our emotions to arise and pass, without getting swept away by them or identifying with them.

Acceptance is the willingness to acknowledge and make peace with our present reality, however challenging it may be. It's about surrendering to what is, rather than fighting against it, and finding serenity in the midst of chaos. By cultivating a mindset of acceptance, we can free ourselves from the grip of fear and resistance, allowing space for growth and transformation to unfold.

Acceptance does not mean resignation or passivity. Rather, it's about acknowledging the truth of our situation – both the pleasant and the unpleasant aspects – and making a conscious choice to embrace it with openness and equanimity. This doesn't mean that we have to like or condone our circumstances, but rather that we're willing to meet them with courage and grace, trusting in our ability to navigate them with resilience and resilience.

Building a Support Network

Human connection is a cornerstone of emotional resilience. Having a supportive network of friends, family, and mentors can provide us with a sense of belonging, validation, and emotional support during difficult times. It's important to nurture these relationships and reach out for help when we need it, rather than trying to go it alone.

Building a support network also involves fostering relationships with individuals who inspire and uplift us. Surrounding ourselves with positive influences can help us maintain perspective and resilience in the face of adversity. Whether it's a trusted friend, a supportive colleague, or a compassionate therapist, having someone to lean on can make all the difference in our ability to weather life's storms.

Moreover, building a support network entails setting boundaries and prioritizing our own well-being. It's important to surround ourselves with people who respect and validate our experiences, rather than invalidate or dismiss them. By cultivating relationships based on mutual respect and empathy, we can create a supportive environment in which we feel valued, understood, and accepted for who we are.

Finding Meaning and Purpose in Adversity

Adversity has a way of stripping away the superficialities of life and revealing what truly matters to us. It's during these dark nights of the soul that we're called to confront life's deepest questions and search for meaning and purpose amidst the chaos. Finding meaning in adversity is not about denying or minimizing our pain but rather transcending it and discovering the lessons and blessings that lie hidden within.

Finding meaning can involve reframing our perspective, seeing challenges as opportunities for growth and learning. It can also involve aligning our actions with our values and purpose, channeling our struggles into meaningful pursuits that contribute to the greater good. By finding meaning in adversity, we can transform our suffering into a source of strength and resilience, allowing us to emerge from the darkness with newfound clarity and purpose.

In conclusion, cultivating emotional resilience is a lifelong journey that requires practice, patience, and self-compassion. By developing awareness of our emotions, practicing self-regulation, nurturing supportive relationships, and finding meaning in adversity, we can cultivate the inner resources necessary to navigate life's inevitable ups and downs with grace and resilience. As Robert Frost reminds us, "The only way out is through." By embracing our emotions and facing our challenges head-on, we can emerge stronger and more resilient on the other side.

Chapter 03

Nurturing Physical Resilience

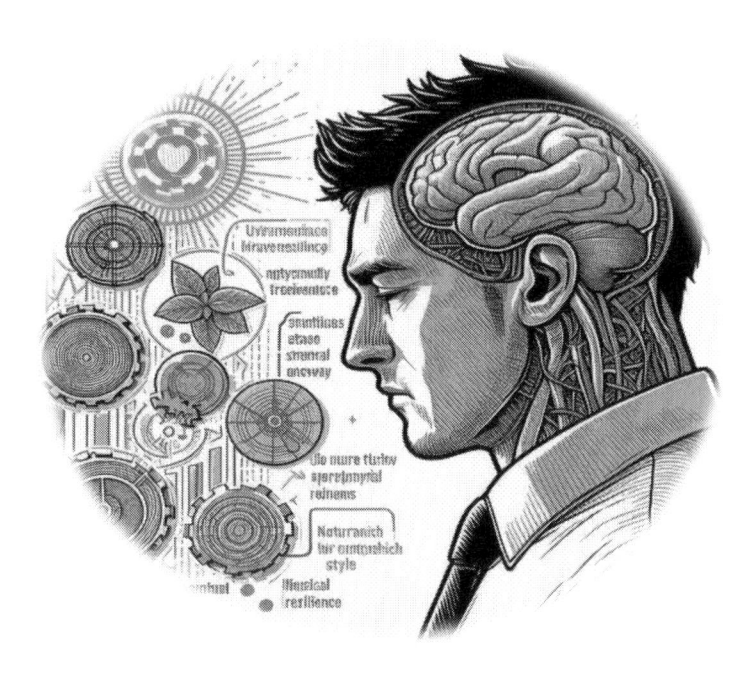

"In the midst of movement and chaos, keep stillness inside of you." - Deepak Chopra

Physical resilience forms the foundation of our ability to withstand the challenges of turbulent times. When our bodies are strong and healthy, we're better equipped to cope with stress, bounce back from setbacks, and maintain a sense of equilibrium amidst chaos. In this chapter, we'll explore strategies for nurturing physical resilience, focusing on self-care, exercise, sleep, and nutrition.

Prioritizing Self-Care and Wellness

Self-care is the cornerstone of physical resilience. It involves making intentional choices to prioritize our health and well-being, even in the midst of busy and demanding schedules. Self-care encompasses a wide range of activities, from simple acts of kindness toward ourselves to more structured practices aimed at promoting physical and mental health.

Self-care can take many forms, depending on our individual preferences and needs. It might involve carving out time for relaxation and leisure activities, such as reading, meditating, or spending time in nature. It could also involve seeking professional support, such as therapy or counseling, to address underlying issues and promote emotional well-being.

The key to effective self-care is consistency and balance. It's about finding activities that nourish and rejuvenate us, rather than deplete or drain us. By prioritizing self-care as an integral part of our daily routine, we can cultivate physical resilience and create a solid foundation for navigating life's challenges with grace and ease.

Incorporating Exercise and Movement into Daily Routines

Regular exercise is essential for maintaining physical resilience. Not only does it strengthen our muscles and improve our cardiovascular health, but it also boosts our mood, reduces stress, and enhances our overall sense of well-being. Incorporating exercise into our daily routines is a powerful way to build resilience and fortify our bodies against the demands of everyday life.

Exercise doesn't have to be complicated or time-consuming to be effective. Even small amounts of physical activity can have significant benefits for our health and resilience. Whether it's taking a brisk walk during our lunch break, practicing yoga in the morning, or dancing to our favorite music in the evening, finding activities that we enjoy and can sustain over time is key to reaping the rewards of regular exercise.

Moreover, variety is the spice of life when it comes to exercise. Mixing up our routine with a combination of cardiovascular, strength training, and flexibility exercises can help prevent boredom and burnout, while also targeting different aspects of physical fitness. By finding activities that we enjoy and can stick with, we can make exercise a sustainable and enjoyable part of our daily lives.

Establishing Healthy Sleep Habits

Quality sleep is essential for physical resilience. It's during sleep that our bodies repair and regenerate, consolidating memories, regulating hormones, and restoring energy levels for the day ahead. Yet, in today's fast-paced world, sleep is often overlooked or sacrificed in favor of productivity and convenience. Establishing healthy sleep habits is crucial for promoting resilience and well-being.

Creating a conducive sleep environment is the first step toward better sleep. This might involve dimming the lights, reducing noise and distractions, and setting a comfortable temperature in the bedroom. It's also important to establish a consistent sleep schedule, going to bed and waking up at the same time each day, even on weekends.

Additionally, practicing relaxation techniques before bed can help signal to our bodies that it's time to wind down and prepare for sleep. Activities such as reading, taking a warm bath, or practicing deep breathing exercises can help calm the mind and promote relaxation, making it easier to fall asleep and stay asleep throughout the night.

Fueling the Body with Nourishing Foods

Nutrition plays a central role in physical resilience. The foods we eat provide the building blocks for our bodies, influencing everything from our energy levels to our immune function. Eating a balanced and nourishing diet is essential for promoting resilience and vitality, especially during times of stress and uncertainty.

Aim to fill your plate with a variety of whole foods,

including fruits, vegetables, whole grains, lean proteins, and healthy fats. These foods are rich in essential nutrients, such as vitamins, minerals, and antioxidants, which support overall health and well-being. Avoid or limit processed foods, sugary snacks, and refined carbohydrates, which can contribute to inflammation and undermine resilience.

Moreover, staying hydrated is essential for maintaining physical resilience. Aim to drink plenty of water throughout the day, and limit consumption of sugary drinks and alcohol, which can dehydrate the body and impair cognitive function. Herbal teas, infused water, and coconut water are all excellent options for staying hydrated and supporting overall health.

In conclusion, nurturing physical resilience is essential for navigating turbulent times with grace and ease. By prioritizing self-care and wellness, incorporating exercise and movement into daily routines, establishing healthy sleep habits, and fueling the body with nourishing foods, we can create a solid foundation for resilience and well-being. As Deepak Chopra reminds us, "In the midst of movement and chaos, keep stillness inside of you." By cultivating physical resilience, we can maintain our inner calm and strength, even in the face of life's storms.

Chapter 04

Strengthening Mental Resilience

"It is not the strongest of the species that survives, nor the most intelligent, but the one most responsive to change." - Charles Darwin

In the face of adversity, our mental resilience becomes our greatest asset. Mental resilience empowers us to adapt, persevere, and thrive amidst challenges, allowing us to emerge from difficult situations stronger and more resilient than before. In this chapter, we will explore strategies for strengthening mental resilience, drawing on insights from psychology, neuroscience, and personal development.

Cultivating a Growth Mindset

At the heart of mental resilience lies a growth mindset – the belief that our abilities and intelligence can be developed through effort, perseverance, and learning. Cultivating a growth mindset involves shifting from a fixed mindset, which views abilities as innate and unchangeable, to a growth mindset, which sees challenges as opportunities for growth and learning.

A growth mindset is characterized by resilience, optimism, and a willingness to embrace failure as a natural part of the learning process. It's about reframing setbacks as temporary setbacks rather than insurmountable obstacles and seeing feedback as an opportunity for improvement rather than criticism.

Practicing cognitive reframing and positive self-talk is essential for cultivating a growth mindset. When faced with challenges or setbacks, rather than succumbing to self-doubt or negativity, we can choose to reframe our perspective and focus on the opportunities for growth and learning. By replacing negative self-talk with positive affirmations and encouragement, we can build resilience and confidence in our ability to overcome obstacles.

Moreover, developing a growth mindset involves embracing challenges as opportunities for growth and learning. Rather than avoiding difficulties or seeking easy paths, we can lean into challenges, recognizing them as opportunities to stretch ourselves, acquire new skills, and expand our capabilities. By approaching challenges with a sense of curiosity and openness, rather than fear or avoidance, we can cultivate resilience and adaptability in the face of adversity.

Engaging in Continuous Learning and Skill Development

Continuous learning is key to maintaining mental resilience in the face of change and uncertainty. By expanding our knowledge and skills, we can adapt to new challenges, seize opportunities, and stay ahead of the curve in an ever-evolving world. Whether it's learning a new language, mastering a musical instrument, or acquiring new professional skills, engaging in lifelong learning fosters adaptability and resilience.

Moreover, skill development goes hand in hand with mental resilience. By honing our abilities and expertise in areas relevant to our goals and aspirations, we can enhance our confidence, competence, and resilience in the face of adversity. Setting aside time for deliberate practice and skill development each day, even if it's just a few minutes, can yield significant benefits over time.

Continuous learning also involves seeking feedback

and constructive criticism from others. Rather than viewing feedback as a threat to our ego, we can see it as an opportunity for growth and improvement. By embracing feedback with an open mind and a willingness to learn, we can identify areas for development and take proactive steps to enhance our skills and capabilities.

Leveraging Adversity as an Opportunity for Personal Growth

Adversity has a way of revealing our inner strengths and capabilities. Rather than seeing challenges as roadblocks to our success, we can choose to view them as opportunities for personal growth and development. Adversity invites us to dig deep, to tap into our resilience and resourcefulness, and to emerge from difficult situations stronger and more resilient than before.

Leveraging adversity as an opportunity for personal growth involves reframing our perspective and focusing on the lessons and blessings that arise from difficult situations. It's about adopting a mindset of curiosity and openness, rather than fear and resistance, and embracing the journey of self-discovery and transformation that adversity offers.

Moreover, resilience is not just about bouncing back from adversity but also about bouncing forward – using the lessons learned and experiences gained to propel us toward our goals and aspirations. By leveraging adversity as a catalyst for personal growth, we can turn setbacks into stepping stones and challenges into opportunities for greater resilience, wisdom, and fulfillment.

In conclusion, strengthening mental resilience is essential for navigating the challenges of life with grace and courage. By cultivating a growth mindset, practicing cognitive reframing and positive self-talk, engaging in continuous learning and skill development, and leveraging adversity as an opportunity for personal growth, we can build the inner resources necessary to thrive amidst change and uncertainty. As Charles Darwin reminds us, "It is not the strongest of the species that survives, nor the most intelligent, but the one most responsive to change." By cultivating mental resilience, we can adapt and thrive in an ever-changing world.

Chapter 05
Fostering Social Resilience

"Alone, we can do so little; together, we can do so much." - Helen Keller

Social resilience forms the backbone of our ability to weather life's storms with grace and fortitude. In times of adversity, our connections with others serve as lifelines, providing us with support, strength, and solidarity. In this chapter, we will delve deeper into strategies for fostering social resilience, drawing on principles of community building, mutual aid, and collective well-being.

Building and Maintaining Supportive Relationships

The foundation of social resilience lies in the strength of our interpersonal connections. Building and maintaining supportive relationships with friends, family, colleagues, and neighbors is essential for weathering life's challenges with resilience and courage. These relationships offer us a sense of belonging, validation, and emotional support, providing a cushion against the harshness of adversity.

To cultivate supportive relationships, it's essential to invest time and effort in nurturing connections with others. This might involve reaching out to friends and loved ones regularly, checking in on how they're doing, and offering a listening ear and a shoulder to lean on when needed. Authenticity and vulnerability are key in fostering deep and meaningful connections that withstand the test of time and adversity.

Furthermore, building a diverse network of relationships enriches our social resilience. By cultivating connections with individuals from different backgrounds, cultures, and experiences, we broaden our understanding of the world and gain new insights into our own challenges and struggles. Diversity in our social networks exposes us to a variety of perspectives and resources, enhancing our resilience and adaptability.

Contributing to Community and Collective Well-being

Social resilience isn't just about receiving support from others; it's also about contributing to the well-being of our communities and the collective. Actively participating in community life and volunteering our time and talents to support others not only strengthens our social ties but also fosters a sense of purpose and belonging that enhances our resilience.

Contributing to community and collective well-being can take many forms, depending on our interests, skills, and resources. It might involve volunteering at a local soup kitchen, participating in neighborhood clean-up efforts, or organizing a fundraiser for a cause we believe in. By giving back to others and contributing to the greater good, we cultivate a sense of connection and solidarity that bolsters our resilience in times of adversity.

Moreover, contributing to collective well-being empowers us and fosters a sense of agency. It reminds us that we have the power to make a positive difference in the world, even in the face of daunting challenges. By taking action to address social issues and support marginalized communities, we not only strengthen our resilience but also create a more just and equitable society for all.

Seeking and Offering Help When Needed

Central to social resilience is the willingness to seek and offer help when needed. In times of crisis or adversity, reaching out for support can be a powerful act of resilience, reminding us that we're not alone in our struggles and that it's okay to ask for help. Similarly, offering help to others in need strengthens our social bonds and reinforces our sense of connection and belonging.

Seeking help when needed requires vulnerability and courage, as it involves admitting that we're struggling and reaching out to others for support. This might involve confiding in a trusted friend, family member, or mental health professional, or seeking support from a support group or community organization. By reaching out for help, we not only lighten our own burden but also create opportunities for deeper connection and support from others.

Offering help to others in need is equally important for fostering social resilience. Whether it's offering a listening ear to a friend in distress, providing practical assistance to a neighbor in need, or volunteering our time and resources to support a community initiative, acts of kindness and compassion strengthen our social bonds and reinforce our sense of connection and belonging.

Creating Networks of Trust and Reciprocity

Central to social resilience is the creation of networks of trust and reciprocity - communities in which individuals can rely on one another for support, collaboration, and mutual aid. Building trust within our social networks is essential for fostering resilience, as it creates a foundation of mutual respect and understanding that enables individuals to lean on one another in times of need.

Creating networks of trust and reciprocity involves fostering open communication, transparency, and honesty in our interactions with others. It's about being reliable and trustworthy, keeping our word, and following through on our commitments. By cultivating trust within our social networks, we create a safe and supportive environment in which individuals can turn to one another for support and guidance.

Moreover, reciprocity is key to sustaining social resilience over the long term. By offering support to others when they need it and being willing to receive support in return, we create a culture of mutual aid and solidarity that strengthens our resilience as a community. Reciprocal relationships are based on the principle of give and take, with individuals supporting one another in times of need and celebrating one another's successes and achievements.

In conclusion, fostering social resilience is essential for building strong, supportive communities that can weather life's storms with grace and courage. By building and maintaining supportive relationships, contributing to community and collective well-being, seeking and offering help when needed, and creating networks of trust and reciprocity, we can cultivate the social bonds and connections that strengthen our resilience and enable us to thrive amidst change and uncertainty. As Helen Keller reminds us, "Alone, we can do so little; together, we can do so much." By fostering social resilience, we can build communities that support and uplift one another, even in the face of adversity.

Strategies for Renewal

Chapter 06

Finding Balance in Chaos

"In the chaos, build a temple of love." - Marty Rubin

In the tumultuous currents of life, finding equilibrium becomes imperative for our mental, emotional, and spiritual well-being. This chapter will extensively explore strategies for attaining balance amidst chaos, rooted in principles of self-awareness, mindfulness, and intentional living.

Establishing Boundaries and Priorities

The initial stride towards balance amidst chaos entails delineating clear boundaries and discerning priorities. When buffeted by the swirling winds of demands and obligations, it's effortless to feel overwhelmed and fragmented. By delineating our boundaries and identifying our priorities, we can channel our time and energy towards endeavors that resonate deeply with our values and aspirations.

Establishing boundaries necessitates the ability to gracefully decline activities, commitments, and relationships that deplete our energy or divert our focus from what truly matters. It involves setting limits on our time and resources and intentionally allocating them to activities that align with our values and goals. By prioritizing our well-being and nurturing relationships that nourish and uplift us, we cultivate a sense of clarity and purpose that guides our decisions and actions.

Moreover, setting boundaries is pivotal for safeguarding our mental and emotional health. It empowers us to honor our needs and limitations without succumbing to guilt or succumbing to the pressure to please others at the expense of our well-being. By asserting our boundaries assertively and compassionately, we create space for self-care, creativity, and rejuvenation amidst the whirlwind of life's chaos.

Practicing Mindfulness and Presence

Mindfulness emerges as an invaluable tool for discovering balance amidst chaos. It entails fostering awareness of our thoughts, emotions, and sensations in the present moment, sans judgment or attachment. Through mindfulness, we ground ourselves in the immediacy of the present, fostering a state of tranquility and lucidity that facilitates navigation through life's vicissitudes with resilience and equanimity.

Mindfulness manifests in myriad forms, spanning from formal meditation to the infusion of mindfulness into everyday activities such as walking, eating, or even breathing. It involves directing our full attention and awareness to our current experience, unfettered by rumination or preoccupation with past or future concerns. By anchoring ourselves in the present moment, we mitigate stress, anxiety, and overwhelm, thereby fostering serenity and contentment amidst the tumult of chaos.

Incorporating Moments of Rest and Reflection

Amidst the tempest of chaos, it proves imperative to carve out intervals of rest and reflection to replenish and revitalize our energy reservoirs. Rest transcends mere physical repose; it encompasses mental, emotional, and spiritual rejuvenation. It necessitates granting ourselves permission to decelerate, pause, and nourish ourselves holistically.

Incorporating moments of rest and reflection may assume myriad forms, contingent on our predilections and exigencies. It might entail interspersing short intervals throughout the day for stretching, deep breathing, or simply basking in stillness. Alternatively, it could encompass engaging in activities that imbue us with joy and tranquility, such as reading, immersing ourselves in nature, or practicing creative pursuits.

Reflection serves as an indispensable companion to rest in our quest for balance amidst chaos. It entails dedicating time to contemplate our experiences, thoughts, and emotions, thereby gleaning insight into our inner landscape and aspirations. Reflection enables us to attain perspective on our challenges and triumphs, identify avenues for growth and transformation, and chart a course towards fulfillment and authenticity. By embracing moments of rest and reflection, we replenish our vitality and clarity, thus approaching life's tumult with renewed vigor and resilience.

Seeking Harmony Amidst Chaos

Ultimately, the pursuit of balance amidst chaos embodies the quest for harmony – a state of holistic alignment and integration that transcends external turmoil. Harmony does not entail eradicating chaos or attaining flawless equilibrium; rather, it encompasses embracing life's flux with grace and acceptance. It entails discovering beauty and meaning amidst chaos, fostering resilience and equanimity in the face of adversity.

Seeking harmony entails aligning our actions with our values and priorities, and leading lives imbued with intentionality and purpose. It necessitates navigating the delicate balance between endeavor and surrender, between striving for progress and surrendering to the flow of life. By embracing the paradoxes inherent in existence and holding space for both chaos and tranquility, we unearth equilibrium amidst the maelstrom, and traverse life's vicissitudes with grace and courage.

In conclusion, finding balance amidst chaos is imperative for fostering our holistic well-being and resilience amidst the vicissitudes of life. By establishing boundaries and priorities, practicing mindfulness and presence, incorporating moments of rest and reflection, and seeking harmony amidst chaos, we cultivate a sense of equilibrium that empowers us to thrive amidst life's tumult. As Marty Rubin sagely observed, "In the chaos, build a temple of love." By cultivating balance and harmony amidst chaos, we construct sanctuaries of peace and resilience within ourselves, enabling us to navigate life's storms with grace and fortitude.

Chapter 07

Embracing Change

"Change is the only constant in life." -
Heraclitus

Change is an inexorable force, weaving through the fabric of our existence, reshaping our realities, and sculpting our destinies. In this chapter, we embark on a profound exploration of the art of embracing change as a conduit for growth, transformation, and self-realization. Drawing upon the wisdom of ancient sages and modern scholars, we unravel the intricacies of relinquishing resistance, perceiving change as an opportunity for growth, adapting flexibly to new circumstances, and greeting uncertainty with courage and curiosity.

Letting Go of Resistance to Change

Resistance to change manifests as a formidable barrier, impeding our capacity to embrace the dynamic flux of life with grace and resilience. It stems from a primal impulse to cling to familiarity, security, and predictability, even as the tides of change surge around us. However, the more fervently we resist change, the more we prolong our suffering and impede our capacity for growth and adaptation.

Letting go of resistance to change necessitates cultivating an ethos of acceptance and surrender – a willingness to release our grip on the past and immerse ourselves in the unfolding mystery of the present moment. It beckons us to reframe change not as an adversary to be vanquished but as a companion on the journey of self-discovery and transformation.

Furthermore, letting go of resistance to change mandates confronting our deepest fears, insecurities, and attachments with compassionate awareness. It calls upon us to relinquish the illusion of control and entrust ourselves to the uncharted currents of the unknown. By summoning the courage to relinquish resistance and embrace change with open arms, we liberate ourselves to explore the boundless realms of possibility and potentiality that lie beyond the horizon of our comfort zone.

Viewing Change as an Opportunity for Growth

Change, despite its disquieting visage, harbors within its chrysalis the promise of renewal, evolution, and metamorphosis. Rather than cowering in trepidation at the prospect of change, we have the opportunity to reframe it as a sacred crucible for personal and collective growth.

Viewing change as an opportunity for growth invites us to adopt a mindset of curiosity and receptivity – an eagerness to embrace the mysteries and wonders that lie concealed within the labyrinth of transformation. It beseeches us to perceive change not as a harbinger of chaos but as a catalyst for innovation, creativity, and self-realization.

Moreover, viewing change as an opportunity for growth compels us to cultivate resilience – the capacity to rebound from adversity, to transmute setbacks into stepping stones, and to transfigure challenges into catalysts for empowerment. By reframing change as an invitation to expand our horizons, deepen our insights, and actualize our latent potential, we harness its transformative power to propel us towards the summits of self-actualization and fulfillment.

Adapting Flexibly to New Circumstances

Adaptability emerges as the cornerstone of resilience, enabling us to navigate the labyrinthine twists and turns of life with nimbleness, agility, and fortitude. In an era characterized by unprecedented volatility, uncertainty, complexity, and ambiguity (VUCA), the ability to adapt flexibly to new circumstances assumes paramount significance.

Adapting flexibly to new circumstances entails cultivating a growth mindset – a belief in our inherent capacity for learning, growth, and adaptation in response to the vicissitudes of change. It compels us to transcend the shackles of rigidity and dogma, to embrace the fluidity and malleability of existence, and to cultivate an ethos of continuous evolution and self-transcendence.

Furthermore, adapting flexibly to new circumstances mandates staying attuned to the rhythms and nuances of our inner landscape – tuning into the whispers of intuition, discernment, and wisdom that emanate from the depths of our being. It beckons us to trust in the inherent wisdom of the evolutionary impulse that animates all of creation, guiding us towards alignment with the cosmic currents of transformation.

Embracing Uncertainty with Courage and Curiosity

Uncertainty, with its enigmatic allure, often evokes trepidation and apprehension in the recesses of our psyche. Yet, within the crucible of uncertainty lies the crucible of alchemical transmutation, wherein the base metal of fear is transmuted into the golden elixir of courage, resilience, and growth.

Embracing uncertainty with courage and curiosity entails cultivating a spirit of radical acceptance – a willingness to surrender to the unknowable mysteries of existence and to dance with the divine chaos that swirls around us. It implores us to relinquish the illusion of security and certainty, and to greet the uncharted terrain of the unknown with an open heart and mind.

Furthermore, embracing uncertainty with courage and curiosity calls forth the indomitable spirit of the adventurer – the intrepid explorer who dares to venture beyond the confines of the familiar and immerse themselves in the uncharted realms of possibility and potentiality. It invites us to navigate the labyrinth of uncertainty with fortitude, resilience, and an insatiable thirst for discovery.

In conclusion, the journey of embracing change unfolds as a sacred odyssey of self-discovery, transformation, and transcendence. By letting go of resistance, viewing change as an opportunity for growth, adapting flexibly to new circumstances, and embracing uncertainty with courage and curiosity, we harness the transformative power of change to sculpt the contours of our destiny and to embark upon the path of self-realization and fulfillment. As Heraclitus so sagely proclaimed, "Change is the only constant in life." By embracing change, we awaken to the boundless potentiality that resides within the crucible of transformation, and we emerge reborn, resplendent, and radiant with the luminous light of infinite possibility.

Chapter 08

Cultivating Gratitude

"Gratitude unlocks the fullness of life." - Melody Beattie

Gratitude, often described as the sweet nectar of the soul, is a transformative force that has the power to illuminate even the darkest corners of our existence. In this chapter, we embark on a profound journey into the heart of gratitude, exploring its myriad facets and uncovering the profound impact it can have on our lives. Drawing inspiration from the timeless wisdom of Melody Beattie and other luminaries, we delve into the art of cultivating gratitude as a daily practice, a shift in perspective, and a source of boundless joy and abundance.

Practicing Daily Gratitude Rituals

At its core, gratitude is a practice—an intentional, conscious choice to cultivate appreciation and thankfulness for the blessings that grace our lives each day. Practicing daily gratitude rituals provides us with an opportunity to pause, reflect, and attune our hearts to the abundance that surrounds us, even in the midst of life's challenges.

Daily gratitude rituals can take many forms, each tailored to suit our unique preferences and circumstances. Some may find solace in keeping a gratitude journal, where they can jot down three things they're thankful for each day. Others may prefer to create a gratitude altar adorned with symbols of abundance and blessings, or to simply take a few moments each morning to offer silent thanks for the gift of life itself.

By infusing our daily lives with the practice of gratitude,

we elevate our consciousness, cultivate a sense of presence, and open ourselves to receive the blessings that flow effortlessly into our lives.

Shifting Perspective to Focus on Abundance Rather Than Scarcity

In a world often characterized by scarcity and lack, the practice of gratitude invites us to shift our perspective and behold the abundance that surrounds us in every moment. Instead of fixating on what we lack or yearning for what lies beyond our grasp, gratitude empowers us to recognize and celebrate the richness and fullness of life in all its myriad hues.

Shifting our perspective to focus on abundance rather than scarcity involves a conscious recalibration of our mental and emotional lenses — a willingness to see the glass as half full rather than half empty, to count our blessings rather than our burdens, and to savor the richness and fullness of life in all its myriad hues.

Moreover, cultivating an attitude of abundance empowers us to transcend the limitations of scarcity consciousness and embrace a mindset of prosperity and generosity. By acknowledging the infinite reservoir of blessings that flows ceaselessly into our lives, we align ourselves with the cosmic currents of abundance and invite prosperity to manifest in ever-expanding circles of grace and gratitude.

Recognizing the Blessings Within Challenges

Even amidst life's most formidable challenges and adversities, the seeds of gratitude lie waiting to be discovered, nurtured, and cultivated. By embracing a perspective of radical acceptance and unconditional gratitude, we unlock the hidden blessings concealed within the crucible of adversity and transform our trials into triumphs.

Recognizing the blessings within challenges entails a willingness to look beyond the surface level of pain and suffering and discern the deeper lessons and gifts that lie concealed beneath the surface. It's about embracing our struggles as opportunities for growth, resilience, and transformation and recognizing that even in the darkest moments, there exists a glimmer of light and hope.

Furthermore, cultivating gratitude amidst challenges empowers us to reclaim our agency and sovereignty in the face of adversity. By reframing our struggles as catalysts for personal and spiritual evolution, we transcend the victim mentality and step into our inherent power as co-creators of our destiny.

Expressing Appreciation and Kindness Towards Others

Gratitude, when expressed and shared, amplifies its potency and radiance, infusing our relationships with warmth, connection, and harmony. Expressing appreciation and kindness towards others serves as a powerful catalyst for deepening our bonds, fostering a culture of generosity and reciprocity, and spreading waves of love and gratitude throughout the tapestry of human experience.

Expressing appreciation and kindness towards others can take myriad forms, from offering heartfelt words of thanks and praise to performing acts of kindness and compassion. It's about acknowledging the contributions and sacrifices of others, celebrating their triumphs and successes, and holding space for their vulnerabilities and struggles with empathy and compassion.

Moreover, expressing appreciation and kindness towards others creates a ripple effect of positivity and goodwill that extends far beyond the boundaries of our individual interactions. By sowing seeds of gratitude and kindness in the fertile soil of human connection, we cultivate a world imbued with love, generosity, and abundance—a world where every heart beats in harmony with the cosmic symphony of gratitude and grace.

In conclusion, cultivating gratitude emerges as a sacred alchemical process—a journey of awakening, transformation, and liberation. By practicing daily gratitude rituals, shifting our perspective to focus on abundance rather than scarcity, recognizing the blessings within challenges, and expressing appreciation and kindness towards others, we unlock the fullness of life and awaken to the miraculous tapestry of blessings that unfurls before us in every moment. As Melody Beattie so eloquently proclaimed, "Gratitude unlocks the fullness of life." By cultivating gratitude, we infuse our lives with boundless joy, abundance, and grace, and awaken to the infinite wonders that lie within and around us.

Chapter 09

Harnessing Creativity

"Creativity takes courage." - *Henri Matisse*

In the labyrinth of human existence, creativity stands as a guiding light, illuminating the path of discovery, innovation, and self-expression. This chapter embarks on a profound exploration of creativity, delving into its depths and uncovering the transformative power it holds within. Drawing inspiration from the timeless wisdom of Henri Matisse and other creative visionaries, we embark on a journey to harness creativity as a beacon of exploration, a source of inspiration, and a catalyst for self-realization.

Embracing Experimentation and Exploration

At the nucleus of creativity resides the spirit of experimentation and exploration—a boundless curiosity that propels us beyond the confines of convention and into the uncharted realms of possibility. Embracing experimentation is an invitation to relinquish the fear of failure, to embrace the unknown with open arms, and to embark on a voyage of discovery without the constraints of preconceived notions or self-imposed limitations.

Experimentation liberates us from the shackles of conformity and invites us to dance on the edges of our comfort zone, where growth and transformation flourish. It beckons us to adopt a mindset of playful curiosity, where mistakes are celebrated as stepping stones to innovation, and setbacks are viewed as opportunities for learning and growth.

Exploration, on the other hand, is a journey into the boundless expanse of the imagination—a quest to uncover the hidden gems of inspiration that lie dormant within our souls. It invites us to roam freely through the corridors of possibility, to heed the whispers of intuition, and to follow the winding path of creativity wherever it may lead.

Together, experimentation and exploration awaken us to the infinite potential that resides within, guiding us towards uncharted territories of discovery, innovation, and self-expression.

Cultivating a Playful and Curious Mindset

Creativity thrives in the fertile soil of a playful and curious mindset—a childlike wonder that sees the world with fresh eyes and embraces the joy of discovery at every turn. Cultivating such a mindset requires us to shed the layers of cynicism and skepticism that accumulate with age, and to reconnect with the innocence and spontaneity of our inner child.

A playful mindset invites us to approach life with a sense of lightness and joy, to greet each day with a spirit of adventure and excitement. It encourages us to infuse our daily routines with a sense of whimsy and spontaneity, to seek out moments of laughter and delight amidst the hustle and bustle of modern life.

A curious mindset, on the other hand, is driven by an insatiable hunger for knowledge and understanding— an unquenchable thirst to explore the mysteries of the universe and unlock the secrets of existence. It compels us to ask questions, to challenge assumptions, and to venture into the unknown with an open heart and an inquiring mind.

Together, a playful and curious mindset serves as a gateway to the realms of creativity, inspiring us to see the world with fresh eyes and embrace the boundless possibilities that lie beyond the horizon of our imagination.

Finding Inspiration in Unexpected Places

Inspiration, that elusive muse that whispers in the ear of the creative soul, often reveals itself in the most unexpected of places—in the delicate flutter of a butterfly's wings, the gentle rustle of leaves in the wind, or the radiant hues of a sunset sky. Finding inspiration in unexpected places requires us to cultivate a keen sense of awareness and receptivity, to attune ourselves to the subtle rhythms and nuances of the world around us.

Such inspiration can be found in the beauty of nature, the wisdom of ancient teachings, or the depths of our own inner landscape. It may manifest as a sudden flash of insight, a fleeting moment of clarity, or a profound sense of connection with the world around us.

By opening ourselves to the possibility of inspiration in unexpected places, we expand our perception, deepen our understanding, and infuse our creative endeavors with a sense of vitality and authenticity.

Using Creativity as a Tool for Problem-Solving and Self-Expression

Creativity is not merely a means of artistic expression; it is a powerful tool for problem-solving, innovation, and self-discovery. By harnessing creativity as a tool for problem-solving, we unlock new pathways to understanding, insight, and transformation.

Creative problem-solving involves approaching challenges with an open mind and a willingness to explore unconventional solutions. It requires us to embrace ambiguity and uncertainty, to challenge assumptions, and to think outside the box in search of innovative solutions.

Moreover, creativity serves as a vehicle for self-expression—a canvas upon which we can paint the tapestry of our innermost thoughts, feelings, and desires. Whether through music, art, writing, or dance, creative expression allows us to give voice to our deepest truths, to explore the depths of our soul, and to share our unique perspective with the world.

By using creativity as a tool for problem-solving and self-expression, we unlock the full potential of our creative genius, unleashing a torrent of innovation, inspiration, and transformation in our lives and in the world around us.

In conclusion, harnessing creativity is a sacred endeavor—a journey of exploration, discovery, and self-realization. By embracing experimentation and exploration, cultivating a playful and curious mindset, finding inspiration in unexpected places, and using creativity as a tool for problem-solving and self-expression, we unlock the boundless potential that resides within us and awaken to the infinite wonders that lie within and around us. As Henri Matisse so eloquently proclaimed, "Creativity takes courage." By summoning the courage to explore, create, and innovate, we infuse our lives with meaning, purpose, and beauty, and embark on a journey of self-discovery and fulfillment.

Integrating Resilience and Renewal

Chapter 10
Building Resilient Habits

"We are what we repeatedly do. Excellence, then, is not an act, but a habit." - Aristotle

In the intricate tapestry of our lives, habits are the threads that weave together the fabric of our existence. They shape our thoughts, actions, and ultimately, our destinies. This chapter delves into the profound realm of building resilient habits, recognizing their pivotal role in fortifying our capacity for resilience and renewal. Drawing upon the timeless wisdom of Aristotle and other luminaries, we embark on a transformative journey to identify, cultivate, and reinforce habits that support our quest for growth, adaptation, and self-mastery.

Identifying and Reinforcing Positive Habits

Positive habits serve as the cornerstone of resilience and renewal, grounding us amidst life's tumultuous currents and guiding us towards the shores of empowerment and fulfillment. Identifying and reinforcing positive habits requires a deep dive into our inner landscape—an honest examination of our current habits and an exploration of their impact on our overall well-being and flourishing.

Positive habits encompass a vast array of behaviors, spanning physical fitness and self-care to mindfulness and personal development. They may include practices such as regular exercise, nutritious eating, meditation, journaling, and continuous learning. By identifying the habits that nourish our body, mind, and spirit, we lay the foundation for resilience and renewal, cultivating a fertile soil in which the seeds of growth and transformation can flourish.

Reinforcing positive habits entails the deliberate cultivation of discipline and consistency—the willingness to show up day after day, rain or shine, and engage in behaviors that align with our values and aspirations. It demands a commitment to harnessing the power of repetition and routine, transforming fleeting impulses into enduring habits that shape the trajectory of our lives.

Creating Routines that Support Resilience and Renewal

Routines serve as the scaffolding upon which resilient habits are erected, providing structure and stability amidst the ebb and flow of daily life. Crafting routines that support resilience and renewal involves the intentional design of daily rituals and practices that nurture our body, mind, and spirit, fostering a sense of balance and well-being.

These routines may encompass a diverse array of activities tailored to our individual needs and preferences. They might include morning rituals that set the tone for the day ahead, such as meditation, yoga, or gratitude practice; midday breaks for nourishing meals and rejuvenating walks; and evening rituals that promote relaxation and restful sleep, such as reading, reflection, or gentle stretching.

By weaving these practices into the fabric of our daily routines, we cultivate a sense of rhythm and harmony that aligns with the natural cycles of life. We create sacred spaces for self-care and introspection, where we can replenish our energy reserves, nourish our souls, and cultivate resilience in the face of life's inevitable challenges and adversities.

Monitoring Progress and Adapting as Needed

Building resilient habits is not a linear journey; it is a dynamic process of growth and adaptation that unfolds over time. Monitoring progress and adapting as needed involves a commitment to tracking our habits, evaluating their impact on our lives, and making course corrections as necessary to ensure our continued growth and flourishing.

Monitoring progress may take various forms, such as keeping a habit tracker or journal, monitoring key metrics related to our well-being and performance, or seeking feedback from trusted mentors or peers. It requires us to cultivate self-awareness and mindfulness, tuning into the subtle signals and cues that arise within us and using them as guideposts on our journey of self-discovery and transformation.

Moreover, adapting as needed demands a willingness to embrace flexibility and experimentation—the willingness to try new approaches, learn from our mistakes, and pivot in response to changing circumstances. It requires us to release attachment to rigid expectations and outcomes and to embrace the inherent fluidity and unpredictability of life.

Celebrating Small Victories Along the Way

In the pursuit of building resilient habits, it's easy to become fixated on the destination and overlook the beauty of the journey itself. Yet, it is in the small victories and milestones along the way that the true magic of transformation unfolds. Celebrating small victories serves as a powerful reminder of our progress and accomplishments, fueling our motivation and momentum as we continue on our path of growth and renewal.

Celebrating small victories may take myriad forms, from acknowledging our efforts and achievements in a gratitude journal to sharing our successes with loved ones and supporters. It's about taking time to pause, reflect, and savor the moments of triumph and progress that punctuate our journey, infusing our hearts with gratitude and joy.

Moreover, celebrating small victories cultivates a sense of resilience and self-efficacy, bolstering our confidence and belief in our ability to overcome obstacles and achieve our goals. It serves as a beacon of hope and inspiration, reminding us that even in the face of adversity, we possess the strength, resilience, and determination to rise above and thrive.

Embracing Consistency and Persistence

Consistency and persistence are the twin pillars upon which resilient habits are built. They are the steady drumbeat that propels us forward, even in the face of adversity and uncertainty. Embracing consistency involves committing to showing up day after day, rain or shine, and engaging in behaviors that align with our values and aspirations.

Consistency requires us to cultivate a sense of discipline and dedication—to prioritize our well-being and personal growth, even when faced with competing demands and distractions. It's about honoring our commitments to ourselves and others, and staying true to our path, no matter how rocky or challenging it may seem.

Similarly, embracing persistence entails a willingness to persevere in the face of obstacles and setbacks—to summon the courage and resilience to dust ourselves off and keep moving forward, even when the road ahead is steep and winding. It's about harnessing the power of resilience and determination to overcome adversity and realize our dreams and aspirations.

Together, consistency and persistence serve as the bedrock of resilient habits, anchoring us amidst life's tumultuous seas and guiding us towards the shores of empowerment and fulfillment.

Incorporating Mindfulness and Reflection

Mindfulness and reflection are essential companions on the journey of building resilient habits, offering us a sanctuary of stillness and presence amidst the chaos and noise of modern life. Incorporating mindfulness involves cultivating a deep sense of awareness and presence in the present moment, allowing us to observe our thoughts, feelings, and behaviors with clarity and compassion.

Mindfulness practices may include meditation, deep breathing exercises, or mindful movement practices such as yoga or tai chi. They provide us with a refuge from the relentless barrage of stimuli and distractions, allowing us to anchor ourselves in the here and now and cultivate a sense of inner peace and tranquility.

Reflection, on the other hand, invites us to pause and contemplate our experiences, insights, and lessons learned along the journey. It involves carving out sacred space for introspection and self-inquiry, where we can discern the patterns and themes that shape our habits and behaviors and identify areas for growth and improvement.

By incorporating mindfulness and reflection into our daily lives, we deepen our understanding of ourselves and our habits, cultivating greater self-awareness and self-mastery. We become more attuned to the subtle nuances of our inner landscape, and more adept at navigating the twists and turns of our journey with grace and resilience.

Nurturing Self-Compassion and Forgiveness

Self-compassion and forgiveness are essential ingredients in the alchemy of building resilient habits, offering us a gentle embrace in moments of struggle and self-doubt. Nurturing self-compassion involves extending the same kindness, understanding, and acceptance to ourselves that we would offer to a dear friend or loved one.

Self-compassion practices may include self-soothing exercises, loving-kindness meditations, or compassionate self-talk. They provide us with a lifeline of support and solace, reminding us that we are worthy of love and acceptance, regardless of our perceived shortcomings or imperfections.

Similarly, nurturing forgiveness involves releasing ourselves from the burden of past mistakes and transgressions, and embracing the healing power of compassion and reconciliation. It entails acknowledging our humanity, and recognizing that we are all fallible beings who are capable of growth and transformation.

By nurturing self-compassion and forgiveness, we create a nurturing environment for growth and healing, freeing ourselves from the shackles of self-judgment and criticism, and opening our hearts to the boundless possibilities that lie within and around us.

Cultivating a Growth Mindset

A growth mindset is the fertile soil in which resilient habits take root and flourish, offering us a lens through which to view challenges and setbacks as opportunities for growth and learning. Cultivating a growth mindset involves adopting a mindset of curiosity and openness, and reframing failure as a natural and necessary part of the learning process.

A growth mindset is characterized by a belief in our

capacity for change and improvement, and a willingness to embrace challenges and setbacks as stepping stones to success. It empowers us to view obstacles not as insurmountable barriers, but as opportunities to stretch and grow beyond our perceived limitations.

Moreover, cultivating a growth mindset involves fostering a sense of resilience and perseverance in the face of adversity, and cultivating a sense of optimism and possibility that fuels our journey towards our goals and aspirations.

By cultivating a growth mindset, we unlock the door to boundless potential and possibility, and awaken to the infinite possibilities that lie within and around us.

Creating a Supportive Environment

Building resilient habits is not a solitary endeavor; it requires a supportive ecosystem of relationships and environments that nourish and sustain our growth and development. Creating a supportive environment involves surrounding ourselves with individuals who uplift and inspire us, and cultivating spaces that foster creativity, innovation, and self-expression.

A supportive environment may include friends, family members, mentors, and peers who encourage and support us on our journey, and provide us with a safe space to share our struggles, triumphs, and aspirations. It may also include physical spaces such as our home, workplace, or community, that foster a sense of belonging and connection, and provide us with opportunities for growth and collaboration.

By creating a supportive environment, we create a fertile soil in which resilient habits can take root and flourish, and empower ourselves to realize our full potential and purpose in life.

In conclusion, building resilient habits is a sacred journey—a journey of self-discovery, growth, and transformation. By identifying and reinforcing positive habits, creating routines that support resilience and renewal, monitoring progress and adapting as needed, celebrating small victories along the way, embracing consistency and persistence, incorporating mindfulness and reflection, nurturing self-compassion and forgiveness, cultivating a growth mindset, and creating a supportive environment, we unlock the full potential of our being and embark on a path of empowerment and fulfillment. As Aristotle so wisely proclaimed, "We are what we repeatedly do. Excellence, then, is not an act, but a habit." By cultivating resilient habits, we embody the essence of excellence and awaken to the boundless possibilities that lie within and around us.

Chapter 11
Mindfulness in Action

"The present moment is filled with joy and happiness. If you are attentive, you will see it." - Thich Nhat Hanh

In the rush of modern life, amidst the cacophony of competing demands and distractions, lies the sanctuary of the present moment—a wellspring of peace, clarity, and profound insight. This chapter embarks on a journey into the heart of mindfulness, exploring its transformative power and practical application in cultivating resilience and renewal. Drawing inspiration from the timeless wisdom of Thich Nhat Hanh and other mindfulness pioneers, we unravel the mysteries of mindfulness in action, discovering how its practice can illuminate our path, enrich our lives, and awaken us to the boundless possibilities that lie within and around us.

Integrating Mindfulness Practices into Daily Life

Mindfulness is not merely a practice confined to the meditation cushion; it is a way of being—an invitation to bring our full attention and presence to every moment of our lives. Integrating mindfulness practices into daily life involves cultivating a sense of awareness and presence in all that we do, from the mundane to the extraordinary.

Mindfulness practices may take various forms, such as formal meditation, mindful breathing exercises, or body scan practices. They provide us with anchor points in the present moment, allowing us to ground ourselves amidst the turbulence of our thoughts and emotions, and connect with the richness and depth of our lived experience.

Moreover, integrating mindfulness into daily life entails

infusing our daily routines and activities with mindfulness, whether it's eating a meal mindfully, walking mindfully, or engaging in mindful communication with others. It's about cultivating a spirit of attentiveness and receptivity, and embracing each moment with an open heart and mind.

Cultivating Awareness of Thoughts, Emotions, and Sensations

Mindfulness invites us to become intimate observers of our inner landscape—to cultivate a deep sense of awareness and presence in relation to our thoughts, emotions, and sensations. Cultivating awareness involves tuning into the ever-changing stream of thoughts and feelings that arise within us, without judgment or attachment.

Awareness of thoughts allows us to observe the ceaseless chatter of the mind with detachment, recognizing that we are not defined by our thoughts, but rather by the spacious awareness in which they arise and dissolve. Awareness of emotions invites us to embrace the full spectrum of human experience, from joy and gratitude to sadness and anger, with equanimity and compassion. Awareness of sensations grounds us in the embodied experience of the present moment, connecting us with the vitality and aliveness of our physical bodies.

By cultivating awareness of thoughts, emotions, and sensations, we develop a deeper understanding of ourselves and our inner workings, and cultivate greater emotional intelligence and resilience in the face of life's challenges and uncertainties.

Using Mindfulness to Navigate Challenges with Clarity and Composure

Mindfulness is a potent antidote to the myriad stressors and pressures of modern life, offering us a refuge of calm and clarity amidst the storm. Using mindfulness to navigate challenges involves applying the principles of mindfulness—presence, non-reactivity, and acceptance—to difficult situations and emotions.

In times of stress or adversity, mindfulness empowers us to pause, breathe, and ground ourselves in the present moment, rather than getting swept away by the tide of our thoughts and emotions. It enables us to respond to challenges with clarity and composure, rather than reacting impulsively or habitually.

Moreover, mindfulness allows us to cultivate a sense of spaciousness and perspective in the midst of difficulty, enabling us to see challenges as opportunities for growth and learning, rather than insurmountable obstacles. It encourages us to embrace each moment with an open heart and mind, and to meet life's challenges with courage, resilience, and grace.

Harnessing the Power of Presence to Enhance Resilience and Renewal

Presence is the essence of mindfulness—the art of being fully awake and alive to the richness and beauty of each moment. Harnessing the power of presence involves cultivating a deep sense of connection with ourselves, with others, and with the world around us, and infusing our lives with a sense of meaning, purpose, and vitality.

Presence enables us to savor the simple pleasures of life—the warmth of the sun on our skin, the laughter of loved ones, the beauty of a flower in bloom—with awe and appreciation. It allows us to connect with the deeper dimensions of our being—the wisdom of our hearts, the resilience of our spirits, and the interconnectedness of all things—with reverence and gratitude.

Moreover, presence serves as a potent catalyst for resilience and renewal, enabling us to meet life's challenges with openness and equanimity, and to embrace each moment with a sense of curiosity and wonder. It empowers us to navigate the ever-changing currents of existence with grace and resilience, and to awaken to the boundless possibilities that lie within and around us.

In conclusion, mindfulness in action is a sacred journey—a journey of self-discovery, transformation, and awakening. By integrating mindfulness practices into daily life, cultivating awareness of thoughts, emotions, and sensations, using mindfulness to navigate challenges with clarity and composure, and harnessing the power of presence to enhance resilience and renewal, we unlock the full potential of our being and embark on a path of empowerment and fulfillment. As Thich Nhat Hanh so eloquently proclaimed, "The present moment is filled with joy and happiness. If you are attentive, you will see it." By cultivating mindfulness in action, we awaken to the infinite wonders that lie within and around us, and embrace each moment with an open heart and mind.

Chapter 12

Building Inner Strength

"Strength does not come from physical capacity. It comes from an indomitable will." - Mahatma Gandhi

In the crucible of life's trials and tribulations, our inner strength emerges as a steadfast beacon of resilience, fortitude, and unwavering determination. This chapter embarks on a profound exploration of building inner strength, recognizing its transformative power in navigating life's challenges with grace and courage. Drawing upon the timeless wisdom of Mahatma Gandhi and other luminaries, we unravel the mysteries of inner strength, discovering how its cultivation can empower us to weather the storms of adversity and emerge victorious on the other side.

Cultivating Self-Confidence and Self-Efficacy

At the heart of inner strength lies the bedrock of self-confidence and self-efficacy—the unwavering belief in our inherent worth, capabilities, and potential. Cultivating self-confidence involves embracing our unique gifts, talents, and strengths, and trusting in our ability to navigate life's challenges with resilience and grace.

Self-efficacy, on the other hand, entails developing a sense of mastery and competence in our chosen pursuits, and believing in our capacity to achieve our goals and aspirations. It involves setting realistic goals, breaking them down into manageable steps, and taking consistent action towards their attainment.

By cultivating self-confidence and self-efficacy, we

fortify the foundation of our inner strength, empowering ourselves to face life's challenges with courage, conviction, and unwavering determination.

Drawing Upon Inner Resources During Times of Adversity

In the crucible of adversity, our inner strength emerges as a beacon of hope and resilience—a source of courage and fortitude that enables us to withstand life's storms and emerge stronger and more resilient on the other side. Drawing upon inner resources involves tapping into the deep wellspring of wisdom, courage, and resilience that resides within us, and harnessing its transformative power to navigate life's challenges with grace and dignity.

Inner resources may take various forms, such as resilience, courage, faith, and compassion. They provide us with a reservoir of strength and resilience to draw upon in times of need, enabling us to face adversity with courage, grace, and unwavering determination.

Moreover, drawing upon inner resources requires a willingness to cultivate self-awareness and mindfulness—to tune into the subtle nuances of our inner landscape and heed the whispers of intuition and wisdom that arise within us. By cultivating a deep sense of connection with ourselves and our inner resources, we empower ourselves to face life's challenges with clarity, courage, and resilience.

Developing Resilience Muscles Through Practice and Perseverance

Resilience is not a fixed trait but rather a muscle that can be developed and strengthened through practice and perseverance. Developing resilience muscles involves embracing life's challenges as opportunities for growth and learning, and adopting a mindset of curiosity, openness, and resilience in the face of adversity.

Resilience muscles are built through a process of trial and error, perseverance, and self-compassion. They require us to cultivate a willingness to step outside of our comfort zone, confront our fears and limitations, and embrace the unknown with courage and determination.

Moreover, developing resilience muscles involves cultivating a sense of flexibility and adaptability— the willingness to bend but not break in the face of life's challenges, and to embrace change with grace and resilience.

By developing resilience muscles through practice and perseverance, we strengthen the foundation of our inner strength, empowering ourselves to face life's challenges with courage, grace, and unwavering determination.

Recognizing the Inherent Strength Within Oneself

At the core of building inner strength lies the profound recognition of the inherent strength that resides within each and every one of us. It is a recognition that we are not defined by our circumstances or limitations but rather by the indomitable spirit and resilience that lies at the core of our being.

Recognizing the inherent strength within oneself involves cultivating a deep sense of self-acceptance and self-compassion, and acknowledging our worth and value as human beings. It entails embracing our imperfections and vulnerabilities, and recognizing them as sources of strength and resilience rather than weaknesses to be overcome.

Moreover, recognizing the inherent strength within oneself requires a willingness to cultivate a sense of gratitude and appreciation for the blessings and opportunities that abound in our lives. By embracing the fullness of our being and recognizing the inherent strength that lies within us, we empower ourselves to face life's challenges with courage, grace, and unwavering determination.

In conclusion, building inner strength is a sacred journey — a journey of self-discovery, growth, and transformation. By cultivating self-confidence and self-efficacy, drawing upon inner resources during times of adversity, developing resilience muscles through practice and perseverance, and recognizing the inherent strength within oneself, we unlock the full potential of our being and emerge victorious in the face of life's challenges. As Mahatma Gandhi so eloquently proclaimed, "Strength does not come from physical capacity. It comes from an indomitable will." By cultivating inner strength, we awaken to the boundless possibilities that lie within and around us, and embrace each moment with courage, grace, and unwavering determination.

Chapter 13
Navigating Uncertainty

"Life is inherently uncertain. It's a feature, not a bug." - Naval Ravikant

Uncertainty permeates every aspect of our lives, from the mundane to the extraordinary. It is the backdrop against which our stories unfold—a fluid and ever-changing landscape of possibilities, challenges, and opportunities. This chapter delves into the depths of navigating uncertainty, recognizing it as an intrinsic aspect of the human condition. Drawing upon the profound insights of Naval Ravikant and other thought leaders, we embark on a transformative journey to embrace uncertainty, develop tolerance for ambiguity, find comfort in the unknown, and cultivate resilience in the face of unpredictable circumstances.

Embracing Uncertainty as a Natural Part of the Human Experience

Uncertainty is not an aberration or anomaly but rather a fundamental aspect of the human condition. It is woven into the fabric of existence—a natural and inevitable consequence of our finite understanding and the infinite complexity of the universe.

Embracing uncertainty involves relinquishing the illusion of control and surrendering to the inherent unpredictability of life. It entails cultivating a spirit of curiosity and openness, and embracing each moment with wonder and awe, knowing that it holds within it the seeds of infinite possibility and potential.

By embracing uncertainty as a natural part of the human experience, we liberate ourselves from the shackles of fear and anxiety, and open ourselves to the boundless opportunities for growth and transformation that lie within and around us.

Developing Tolerance for Ambiguity

Tolerance for ambiguity is the cornerstone of resilience in the face of uncertainty. It is the capacity to navigate the murky waters of the unknown with courage, clarity, and composure, rather than succumbing to fear or doubt.

Developing tolerance for ambiguity involves cultivating a willingness to embrace complexity and nuance, and to sit with the discomfort of not knowing. It requires us to resist the temptation to seek certainty or closure prematurely, and to remain open to the myriad possibilities and perspectives that arise in the face of uncertainty.

Moreover, developing tolerance for ambiguity requires a willingness to lean into discomfort and uncertainty, rather than avoiding or suppressing it. It involves embracing the inherent messiness of life and trusting in our ability to navigate its twists and turns with resilience and grace.

Finding Comfort in the Unknown

In the midst of uncertainty lies a hidden treasure—a wellspring of wisdom, creativity, and possibility waiting to be discovered. Finding comfort in the unknown involves cultivating a sense of trust and faith in the unfolding of life's journey, and embracing each moment with an open heart and mind.

Finding comfort in the unknown entails relinquishing

the need for certainty or control, and surrendering to the flow of life with humility and grace. It involves cultivating a sense of surrender and acceptance, and trusting in the inherent intelligence and benevolence of the universe to guide us on our path.

Moreover, finding comfort in the unknown requires a willingness to cultivate a sense of presence and mindfulness, and to anchor ourselves in the here and now, rather than dwelling on the uncertainties of the past or future. It involves embracing each moment with gratitude and appreciation, knowing that it holds within it the seeds of infinite possibility and potential.

Cultivating Resilience in the Face of Unpredictable Circumstances

Resilience is the art of bouncing back from adversity and uncertainty with grace, courage, and unwavering determination. Cultivating resilience in the face of unpredictable circumstances involves developing a mindset of resilience and adaptability, and embracing each challenge as an opportunity for growth and learning.

Cultivating resilience requires us to cultivate a sense of inner strength and fortitude, and to trust in our ability to overcome obstacles and adversity with grace and dignity. It involves developing a mindset of flexibility and adaptability, and embracing change as a natural and inevitable part of the human experience.

Moreover, cultivating resilience requires a willingness to cultivate self-compassion and self-care, and to prioritize our well-being and emotional health amidst life's challenges. It involves reaching out for support and guidance when needed, and cultivating a sense of connection and community with others who can uplift and support us on our journey.

Nurturing Adaptive Capacity

Adaptive capacity is the cornerstone of navigating uncertainty with grace and resilience. It is the capacity to respond to change and uncertainty with agility, creativity, and resourcefulness, rather than rigidity or resistance.

Nurturing adaptive capacity involves cultivating a mindset of curiosity and openness, and embracing change as a natural and inevitable part of the human experience. It requires us to remain flexible and agile in the face of uncertainty, and to embrace new opportunities and possibilities with enthusiasm and optimism.

Moreover, nurturing adaptive capacity entails developing a willingness to learn and grow from our experiences, and to view setbacks and failures as opportunities for growth and learning. It involves cultivating a sense of resilience and perseverance in the face of adversity, and trusting in our ability to overcome obstacles and challenges with grace and dignity.

Cultivating Presence and Mindfulness

Presence and mindfulness are essential allies on the

journey of navigating uncertainty. They offer us a sanctuary of stillness and clarity amidst the chaos and noise of modern life, enabling us to anchor ourselves in the present moment and navigate life's challenges with grace and resilience.

Cultivating presence involves cultivating a deep sense of awareness and attentiveness in the present moment, allowing us to observe our thoughts, feelings, and sensations with clarity and compassion. It entails embracing each moment with an open heart and mind, and cultivating a sense of curiosity and wonder about the mysteries of life.

Mindfulness, on the other hand, involves cultivating a sense of presence and awareness in our everyday activities, from the mundane to the extraordinary. It involves bringing our full attention and intention to each moment, and embracing life's experiences with curiosity, openness, and acceptance.

By cultivating presence and mindfulness, we deepen our capacity to navigate uncertainty with grace and resilience, and awaken to the boundless possibilities that lie within and around us.

Fostering Connection and Community

In the face of uncertainty, connection and community serve as pillars of support and resilience, providing us with a sense of belonging and belongingness that sustains us through life's challenges and adversities. Fostering connection and community involves cultivating meaningful relationships and connections with others, and creating spaces of belonging and inclusion where all are welcome and valued.

Fostering connection and community requires us to cultivate empathy and compassion for others, and to reach out for support and guidance when needed. It involves creating opportunities for collaboration and cooperation, and working together towards shared goals and aspirations.

Moreover, fostering connection and community entails nurturing a sense of belonging and inclusion in our personal and professional lives, and creating spaces where all are welcomed, seen, and valued for who they are.

In conclusion, navigating uncertainty is a sacred journey—a journey of self-discovery, growth, and transformation. By embracing uncertainty as a natural part of the human experience, developing tolerance for ambiguity, finding comfort in the unknown, cultivating resilience in the face of unpredictable circumstances, nurturing adaptive capacity, cultivating presence and mindfulness, and fostering connection and community, we unlock the full potential of our being and emerge victorious in the face of life's challenges. As Naval Ravikant so eloquently proclaimed, "Life is inherently uncertain. It's a feature, not a bug." By embracing uncertainty, we awaken to the infinite possibilities that lie within and around us, and embrace each moment with courage, grace, and unwavering determination.

Chapter 14

Adaptive Leadership

"The art of leadership is saying no, not saying yes. It is very easy to say yes." -
Tony Blair

In the dynamic landscape of today's world, marked by rapid technological advancements, socio-economic shifts, and global disruptions, the role of leadership has evolved into a multifaceted endeavor requiring adaptability, vision, and resilience. Adaptive leadership emerges as a guiding light in navigating the complexities of change, offering a transformative approach that empowers organizations to thrive amidst uncertainty. This chapter delves deeper into the essence of adaptive leadership, exploring its principles, practices, and profound impact on organizational success and sustainability.

Understanding Adaptive Leadership

At its core, adaptive leadership is about leading in the face of ambiguity, complexity, and change. Unlike traditional leadership models that emphasize stability and predictability, adaptive leadership embraces uncertainty as a natural part of the organizational journey and seeks to navigate it with flexibility, agility, and innovation. Adaptive leaders recognize that the challenges of today's world cannot be solved with conventional solutions and instead foster a culture of adaptation and evolution.

Adaptive leadership goes beyond individual charisma or authority; it is a collective endeavor that involves empowering teams and stakeholders to co-create solutions and navigate change together. It requires leaders to listen actively, empathize deeply, and collaborate effectively with diverse perspectives and experiences. By fostering a culture of trust, transparency, and collaboration, adaptive leaders empower their organizations to respond resiliently to external disruptions and seize emerging opportunities.

Leading with Flexibility and Agility

In an era characterized by rapid change and uncertainty, the ability to adapt and pivot quickly is paramount for organizational success. Adaptive leaders lead with flexibility and agility, responding proactively to shifting market dynamics, customer needs, and technological advancements. They recognize that rigid hierarchies and bureaucratic structures hinder innovation and hinder an organization's ability to thrive in a fast-paced environment.

Leading with flexibility and agility involves decentralizing decision-making, empowering teams to experiment and take calculated risks, and fostering a culture of continuous learning and improvement. Adaptive leaders encourage creative problem-solving, embrace diverse perspectives, and challenge the status quo to drive innovation and adaptability. By fostering an environment where individuals are encouraged to voice their ideas and opinions freely, adaptive leaders unleash the collective intelligence of their teams and enable them to navigate change effectively.

Inspiring and Empowering Others to Navigate Change

Adaptive leaders inspire and empower others to navigate change by setting a compelling vision, providing clear direction, and creating a sense of purpose and belonging. They lead by example, demonstrating resilience, optimism, and a willingness to embrace uncertainty. By fostering a shared sense of purpose and direction, adaptive leaders align individual and organizational goals and empower their teams to take ownership of their roles and responsibilities.

Inspiring and empowering others to navigate change involves cultivating a culture of trust, respect, and psychological safety, where individuals feel valued, supported, and encouraged to take risks and innovate. Adaptive leaders invest in developing their team members' skills and capabilities, providing opportunities for growth, learning, and development. They create an environment where individuals feel empowered to challenge the status quo, experiment with new ideas, and learn from failures without fear of judgment or reprisal.

Creating a Culture of Innovation and Experimentation

Innovation is the lifeblood of adaptive organizations, driving growth, competitiveness, and sustainability. Adaptive leaders create a culture of innovation and experimentation that encourages creativity, risk-taking, and continuous improvement. They foster an environment where individuals are encouraged to question assumptions, challenge existing paradigms, and explore new possibilities.

Creating a culture of innovation and experimentation involves removing barriers to creativity and innovation, such as fear of failure, hierarchy, and bureaucracy. Adaptive leaders create space for experimentation, providing resources, support, and encouragement for individuals to test new ideas and approaches. They celebrate successes, learn from failures, and iterate quickly to adapt to changing circumstances and market conditions.

Moreover, creating a culture of innovation and experimentation requires leaders to lead by example, demonstrating a willingness to take risks, embrace uncertainty, and learn from failures. By fostering a culture where innovation is valued, rewarded, and embedded in the organization's DNA, adaptive leaders empower their teams to drive meaningful change and create value for customers, stakeholders, and society at large.

Leveraging Adversity as an Opportunity for Organizational Growth

Adversity is an inevitable part of the organizational journey, presenting challenges, setbacks, and opportunities for growth. Adaptive leaders view adversity not as a roadblock but as a catalyst for innovation, resilience, and transformation. They embrace adversity as an opportunity to learn, grow, and evolve, leveraging it to strengthen the organization's capacity to navigate future challenges.

Leveraging adversity as an opportunity for organizational growth involves reframing setbacks and failures as learning experiences, extracting valuable lessons and insights, and using them to inform future decisions and actions. Adaptive leaders encourage a growth mindset, resilience, and perseverance, fostering a culture where individuals are empowered to bounce back from setbacks with renewed determination and vigor.

Moreover, leveraging adversity as an opportunity for organizational growth requires leaders to provide support, guidance, and resources to help individuals and teams navigate challenges effectively. It involves creating a culture of psychological safety, where individuals feel comfortable taking risks, experimenting with new ideas, and learning from failures without fear of judgment or reprisal.

In conclusion, adaptive leadership is a transformative approach that empowers organizations to thrive in an increasingly complex and uncertain world. By leading with flexibility and agility, inspiring and empowering others to navigate change, creating a culture of innovation and experimentation, and leveraging adversity as an opportunity for growth, adaptive leaders unlock the full potential of their organizations and drive sustainable success and prosperity. As Tony Blair aptly stated, "The art of leadership is saying no, not saying yes." By embracing the principles of adaptive leadership, leaders can navigate change with confidence, vision, and resilience, steering their organizations towards a brighter and more prosperous future.

Chapter 15

Resilient Communication

"The single biggest problem in communication is the illusion that it has taken place." - George Bernard Shaw

Communication is the lifeblood of relationships, both personal and professional. In times of uncertainty and turbulence, resilient communication becomes essential, serving as a bridge that connects individuals and organizations, fosters understanding, and builds trust. This chapter explores the art of resilient communication, delving into the practices and principles that enable individuals and teams to navigate challenges with clarity, empathy, and compassion. Drawing upon the timeless wisdom of George Bernard Shaw and other communication experts, we embark on a journey to uncover the secrets of resilient communication and its transformative power in fostering connection and collaboration.

Practicing Active Listening and Empathy

At the heart of resilient communication lies the art of active listening and empathy. Active listening involves fully engaging with the speaker, tuning into their words, emotions, and body language, and responding with genuine interest and understanding. Empathy, on the other hand, involves putting oneself in the shoes of the other person, seeking to understand their perspective, feelings, and needs.

Practicing active listening and empathy requires setting aside distractions, such as phones or laptops, and giving the speaker your full attention. It involves asking clarifying questions, paraphrasing what you've heard, and validating the speaker's feelings and experiences. By demonstrating empathy and understanding, individuals can foster deeper connections, build trust, and navigate challenges with grace and compassion.

Communicating with Clarity and Transparency

Clear and transparent communication is the cornerstone of resilience in times of uncertainty. It involves conveying information in a straightforward and understandable manner, avoiding jargon or technical language that may confuse or alienate the audience. Transparent communication, on the other hand, entails sharing information openly and honestly, even when the message may be difficult or uncomfortable.

Communicating with clarity and transparency requires careful thought and preparation. It involves considering the needs and perspectives of the audience, tailoring the message to resonate with their interests and concerns, and providing context or background information as needed. By communicating with clarity and transparency, individuals can foster trust, build credibility, and navigate challenges more effectively.

Navigating Difficult Conversations with Grace and Compassion

Difficult conversations are inevitable in both personal and professional settings. Whether addressing performance issues, delivering bad news, or resolving conflicts, navigating difficult conversations requires courage, empathy, and tact. Resilient communication involves approaching these conversations with grace and compassion, seeking to preserve relationships and mutual respect while addressing the underlying issues.

Navigating difficult conversations begins with preparing mentally and emotionally, acknowledging any fears or concerns that may arise. It involves framing the conversation in a constructive and non-confrontational manner, focusing on facts and behaviors rather than personal attacks or judgments. Active listening and empathy are also crucial during difficult conversations, allowing individuals to validate the other person's perspective and feelings while expressing their own.

Building Trust and Rapport Through Effective Communication Strategies

Trust is the foundation of resilient relationships, and effective communication is the key to building and maintaining trust over time. Building trust involves being consistent, reliable, and honest in both words and actions, demonstrating integrity and authenticity in all interactions. Effective communication strategies, such as regular check-ins, open-door policies, and transparent decision-making processes, can help foster trust and rapport within teams and organizations.

Building trust and rapport through effective communication strategies also requires being responsive to feedback and concerns, demonstrating empathy and understanding, and following through on commitments. It involves creating a culture of open communication and collaboration, where individuals feel valued, respected, and empowered to speak up and share their ideas and concerns.

In conclusion, resilient communication is a transformative force that empowers individuals and teams to navigate challenges with clarity, empathy, and compassion. By practicing active listening and empathy, communicating with clarity and transparency, navigating difficult conversations with grace and compassion, and building trust and rapport through effective communication strategies, individuals can foster deeper connections, build stronger relationships, and navigate uncertainty with resilience and grace. As George Bernard Shaw aptly stated, "The single biggest problem in communication is the illusion that it has taken place." By embracing the principles of resilient communication, individuals can bridge the gap between perception and reality, fostering understanding and collaboration in both personal and professional relationships.

Chapter 16

Finding Meaning in Adversity

"Out of difficulties grow miracles." - Jean de La Bruyère

Adversity is an inevitable part of the human experience, presenting challenges, setbacks, and trials that test our resilience and resolve. Yet, amidst the darkness of hardship, there exists an opportunity for profound growth, transformation, and renewal. This chapter delves into the art of finding meaning in adversity, exploring the practices and principles that enable individuals to seek purpose and significance in challenging experiences, transform adversity into opportunities for growth and transformation, find solace and meaning in times of suffering, and use adversity as a catalyst for personal and spiritual development.

Seeking Purpose and Significance in Challenging Experiences

In the face of adversity, finding purpose and significance can provide a beacon of hope and resilience, guiding individuals through the darkest of times. It involves reflecting on one's values, passions, and aspirations, and seeking to align one's actions and decisions with a greater sense of meaning and purpose.

Seeking purpose and significance in challenging experiences requires introspection, self-awareness, and a willingness to explore the deeper meaning behind adversity. It involves asking questions such as "What can I learn from this experience?" and "How can I use this challenge as an opportunity for growth and self-discovery?" By reframing adversity as a potential source of meaning and growth, individuals can transform their relationship with adversity and emerge stronger and more resilient.

Transforming Adversity into Opportunities for Growth and Transformation

Adversity has the power to transform our lives in profound and unexpected ways, catalyzing growth, resilience, and renewal. By embracing adversity as an opportunity for growth and transformation, individuals can cultivate resilience, resourcefulness, and adaptability in the face of life's challenges.

Transforming adversity into opportunities for growth and transformation involves reframing setbacks and failures as learning experiences, and extracting valuable lessons and insights from each challenge. It requires a willingness to step outside of one's comfort zone, and to embrace uncertainty and change with courage and resilience.

Moreover, transforming adversity into opportunities for growth and transformation involves cultivating a mindset of curiosity and openness, and seeking out new experiences and perspectives that challenge and expand our understanding of ourselves and the world around us. By embracing adversity as a catalyst for growth and transformation, individuals can unlock their full potential and emerge stronger and more resilient in the face of life's challenges.

Finding Solace and Meaning in Times of Suffering

In the midst of suffering and hardship, finding solace and meaning can provide comfort and strength, helping individuals navigate the darkest of times with grace and resilience. It involves seeking out sources of support and comfort, such as friends, family, or spiritual communities, and finding ways to connect with others who share similar experiences and struggles.

Finding solace and meaning in times of suffering requires a willingness to confront and acknowledge one's pain and sorrow, and to allow oneself to grieve and heal in a healthy and constructive manner. It involves engaging in practices that promote emotional well-being and self-care, such as mindfulness, meditation, or journaling, and finding moments of beauty and joy amidst the darkness.

Moreover, finding solace and meaning in times of suffering involves reframing adversity as a source of wisdom and compassion, and using one's experiences to cultivate empathy and understanding for others who may be struggling. By finding solace and meaning in times of suffering, individuals can transform their pain into purpose, and emerge stronger and more resilient in the face of life's challenges.

Using Adversity as a Catalyst for Personal and Spiritual Development

Adversity has the power to awaken us to our true

selves, revealing hidden strengths, talents, and qualities that may lie dormant within us. By using adversity as a catalyst for personal and spiritual development, individuals can embark on a journey of self-discovery, growth, and transformation that leads to greater fulfillment and wholeness.

Using adversity as a catalyst for personal and spiritual development involves embracing the lessons and insights that arise from challenging experiences, and using them to inform our choices and actions moving forward. It requires a willingness to confront and transcend our limitations, and to cultivate qualities such as resilience, compassion, and wisdom in the face of adversity.

Moreover, using adversity as a catalyst for personal and spiritual development involves engaging in practices that promote self-awareness, self-reflection, and self-transcendence, such as meditation, prayer, or contemplative practices. By turning inward and connecting with our innermost selves, we can tap into a wellspring of resilience and strength that enables us to navigate life's challenges with grace and dignity.

In conclusion, finding meaning in adversity is a transformative journey—a journey of self-discovery, growth, and renewal. By seeking purpose and significance in challenging experiences, transforming adversity into opportunities for growth and transformation, finding solace and meaning in times of suffering, and using adversity as a catalyst for personal and spiritual development, individuals can emerge stronger, wiser, and more resilient in the face of life's challenges. As Jean de La Bruyère so eloquently proclaimed, "Out of difficulties grow miracles." By embracing the lessons and insights that arise from adversity, individuals can unlock the full potential of their being and emerge victorious in the face of life's challenges.

Chapter 17
Resilient Decision Making

"In any moment of decision, the best thing you can do is the right thing, the next best thing is the wrong thing, and the worst thing you can do is nothing." - Theodore Roosevelt

Decision-making is the cornerstone of progress and growth, shaping the trajectory of our lives and organizations. In today's fast-paced and uncertain world, the ability to make resilient decisions is more critical than ever, enabling individuals and teams to navigate challenges with clarity, confidence, and purpose. This chapter explores the art of resilient decision-making in depth, delving into the principles, strategies, and best practices that empower individuals to make sound decisions in the face of uncertainty and adversity.

Making Decisions with Clarity and Confidence

Decisiveness is a hallmark of effective leadership and resilience. Making decisions with clarity and confidence requires a blend of self-assurance, analytical thinking, and emotional intelligence. It involves assessing the available information, weighing the pros and cons of different options, and choosing a course of action that aligns with one's values, goals, and priorities.

To make decisions with clarity and confidence, individuals must cultivate self-awareness, understanding their strengths, weaknesses, and biases. They must also develop critical thinking skills, honing their ability to analyze complex situations and anticipate potential outcomes. Moreover, they must foster emotional intelligence, recognizing and managing their emotions to make rational decisions even in high-pressure situations.

Furthermore, making decisions with clarity and confidence requires a commitment to continuous learning and growth. Individuals should seek feedback from trusted mentors and colleagues, reflecting on past decisions to identify areas for improvement. By honing their decision-making skills over time, individuals can build the confidence and expertise needed to navigate even the most challenging situations with poise and determination.

Balancing Intuition with Rational Analysis

Resilient decision-making involves striking a delicate balance between intuition and rational analysis. Intuition, often referred to as gut feeling or instinct, is a valuable source of insight that can guide decision-making in uncertain or ambiguous situations. Rational analysis, on the other hand, involves using logic, data, and evidence to assess the merits of different options and predict their likely outcomes.

Balancing intuition with rational analysis requires individuals to trust their instincts while also subjecting them to scrutiny and analysis. It involves paying attention to subtle cues and signals, such as body language or emotional responses, while also considering objective facts and evidence. By integrating intuition and rational analysis, individuals can make more informed and nuanced decisions that reflect both their gut instincts and logical reasoning.

Moreover, balancing intuition with rational analysis requires a willingness to embrace uncertainty and ambiguity. It involves recognizing that not all decisions can be made based on concrete data or evidence, and that sometimes, intuition may be the best guide. By cultivating openness and flexibility in their decision-making process, individuals can leverage both intuition and rational analysis to navigate complex challenges with confidence and clarity.

Learning from Past Mistakes and Failures

Failure is an inevitable part of the journey towards success, and resilient decision-makers recognize that setbacks and mistakes are opportunities for growth and learning. Learning from past mistakes and failures involves adopting a growth mindset, reframing setbacks as valuable learning experiences, and extracting actionable insights that can inform future decisions.

To learn from past mistakes and failures, individuals should conduct a thorough post-mortem analysis, identifying what went wrong and why. They should also reflect on their own role in the decision-making process, considering whether they overlooked key information, succumbed to cognitive biases, or failed to anticipate potential risks. By taking responsibility for their mistakes and seeking to understand their root causes, individuals can avoid repeating the same errors in the future.

Furthermore, learning from past mistakes and failures requires a commitment to continuous improvement and adaptation. Individuals should be open to feedback from others, soliciting input from trusted mentors and colleagues to gain new perspectives on their decision-making process. By embracing a culture of learning and growth, individuals can transform setbacks into stepping stones towards greater resilience and success.

Taking Decisive Action in the Face of Uncertainty

In times of uncertainty and ambiguity, decisive action is often the key to progress and resilience. Resilient decision-makers recognize that indecision and hesitation can be more detrimental than making a wrong decision, and they are willing to take calculated risks and act decisively even when the outcome is uncertain.

Taking decisive action in the face of uncertainty requires courage, conviction, and a willingness to trust one's instincts. It involves weighing the potential risks and benefits of different options, and choosing a course of action that aligns with one's values and objectives. By embracing uncertainty as a natural part of the decision-making process, individuals can make more confident and effective decisions that propel them towards their goals.

Moreover, taking decisive action in the face of uncertainty requires resilience and adaptability. Individuals should be prepared to adjust their course of action as new information emerges or circumstances change, remaining agile and responsive in the face of unexpected challenges. By maintaining a flexible mindset and a willingness to pivot when necessary, individuals can navigate uncertainty with confidence and grace.

In conclusion, resilient decision-making is a foundational skill that empowers individuals and organizations to thrive in an uncertain and ever-changing world. By making decisions with clarity and confidence, balancing intuition with rational analysis, learning from past mistakes and failures, and taking decisive action in the face of uncertainty, individuals can navigate challenges with resilience, courage, and determination. As Theodore Roosevelt aptly stated, "In any moment of decision, the best thing you can do is the right thing, the next best thing is the wrong thing, and the worst thing you can do is nothing." By embracing the principles of resilient decision-making, individuals can overcome obstacles and seize opportunities, charting a course towards a brighter and more prosperous future.

Chapter 18
Adaptive Problem-Solving

"In the middle of difficulty lies opportunity." - Albert Einstein

Problem-solving is a fundamental skill in navigating the complexities of life, both personally and professionally. In today's fast-paced and ever-changing world, the ability to adaptively solve problems is essential for overcoming obstacles, seizing opportunities, and driving innovation. This chapter explores the art of adaptive problem-solving, examining the principles, strategies, and best practices that enable individuals and teams to approach challenges with creativity, resilience, and ingenuity.

Approaching Problems with Creativity and Resourcefulness

Adaptive problem-solving begins with a mindset of creativity and resourcefulness. Instead of viewing problems as insurmountable obstacles, individuals approach them as opportunities for growth, innovation, and learning. Creativity involves thinking outside the box, exploring unconventional solutions, and challenging the status quo. Resourcefulness, on the other hand, involves making the most of available resources, leveraging strengths and talents, and finding creative ways to overcome limitations.

Approaching problems with creativity and resourcefulness requires individuals to cultivate a curious and open-minded mindset. They should be willing to question assumptions, challenge existing paradigms, and explore new possibilities. Moreover, they should be adaptable and flexible, willing to experiment with different approaches and iterate on their ideas based on feedback and outcomes.

Furthermore, approaching problems with creativity and resourcefulness involves collaborating with others and leveraging diverse perspectives and experiences. By tapping into the collective intelligence of teams and organizations, individuals can generate innovative ideas and solutions that transcend individual limitations and propel them towards success.

Breaking Down Complex Challenges into Manageable Tasks

Complex challenges can often feel overwhelming, but adaptive problem-solvers recognize that breaking them down into manageable tasks is the key to success. Instead of trying to tackle the entire problem at once, individuals break it down into smaller, more manageable components, and focus on addressing each one systematically.

Breaking down complex challenges into manageable tasks involves analyzing the problem, identifying its key components and dependencies, and prioritizing them based on their importance and urgency. It also involves setting clear goals and objectives, defining specific tasks and milestones, and developing a structured plan of action to guide the problem-solving process.

Moreover, breaking down complex challenges into manageable tasks requires individuals to be organized, disciplined, and strategic in their approach. They should be able to allocate resources effectively, manage their time and energy efficiently, and monitor their progress towards their goals. By breaking the problem-solving process into smaller, more manageable steps, individuals can maintain momentum and motivation, and overcome obstacles with greater ease and confidence.

Seeking Innovative Solutions to Persistent Problems

Adaptive problem-solving involves seeking innovative solutions to persistent problems, rather than relying on conventional or outdated approaches. It requires individuals to think creatively, challenge assumptions, and explore new possibilities that may not have been considered before.

Seeking innovative solutions to persistent problems involves thinking critically about the root causes of the problem, and identifying opportunities for improvement and innovation. It also involves being open to new ideas and perspectives, and being willing to experiment with different approaches and techniques to find the best solution.

Moreover, seeking innovative solutions to persistent problems requires individuals to be proactive and persistent in their efforts. They should be willing to invest time and resources into researching and testing new ideas, and to persevere in the face of setbacks and challenges. By embracing a mindset of innovation and experimentation, individuals can uncover novel solutions that revolutionize their approach to problem-solving and drive positive change.

Learning from Failures and Adapting Strategies Accordingly

Failure is an inevitable part of the problem-solving process, but adaptive problem-solvers recognize that it is also an opportunity for growth and learning. Instead of viewing failure as a setback, individuals see it as a valuable source of feedback and insight that can inform their future strategies and decisions.

Learning from failures involves conducting a thorough post-mortem analysis, identifying what went wrong and why, and extracting actionable lessons and insights that can be applied to future problem-solving efforts. It also involves being open to feedback and constructive criticism, and being willing to admit when one has made a mistake or overlooked an important consideration.

Moreover, learning from failures involves being adaptable and flexible in one's approach to problem-solving. Individuals should be willing to adjust their strategies and tactics based on new information or changing circumstances, and to experiment with different approaches until they find one that works. By embracing failure as a natural part of the learning process, individuals can build resilience and perseverance, and ultimately become more effective problem-solvers.

In conclusion, adaptive problem-solving is a transformative skill that empowers individuals and teams to overcome obstacles, seize opportunities, and drive innovation. By approaching problems with creativity and resourcefulness, breaking down complex challenges into manageable tasks, seeking innovative solutions to persistent problems, and learning from failures and adapting strategies accordingly, individuals can navigate challenges with confidence, resilience, and ingenuity. As Albert Einstein so aptly stated, "In the middle of difficulty lies opportunity." By embracing the principles of adaptive problem-solving, individuals can transform adversity into opportunity, and chart a course towards success and fulfillment.

Chapter 19
Resilient Relationships

"The quality of your life is the quality of your relationships." - Tony Robbins

Relationships are the cornerstone of human existence, shaping our experiences, emotions, and overall well-being. Resilient relationships serve as pillars of support, offering comfort, companionship, and understanding during life's trials and tribulations. This chapter explores the art of cultivating resilient relationships, examining the principles, strategies, and best practices that enable individuals to foster strong and supportive connections, navigate conflicts and disagreements with empathy and respect, build resilience through effective communication and conflict resolution, and foster mutual trust, respect, and understanding.

Cultivating Strong and Supportive Connections with Others

At the heart of resilient relationships lies the ability to cultivate strong and supportive connections with others. This involves building bonds of trust, empathy, and mutual respect that withstand the test of time and adversity. Cultivating strong and supportive connections requires individuals to invest time and effort into nurturing their relationships, prioritizing communication, and demonstrating genuine care and concern for others.

To cultivate strong and supportive connections with others, individuals should prioritize quality time spent together, engaging in meaningful conversations, shared activities, and acts of kindness that deepen their bond. They should also be proactive in reaching out to others, offering support and encouragement during times of need, and celebrating each other's successes and achievements.

Moreover, cultivating strong and supportive connections with others involves being authentic and vulnerable in one's interactions, sharing one's thoughts, feelings, and experiences openly and honestly. By fostering a culture of trust and transparency within their relationships, individuals can create a safe and nurturing environment where they feel valued, understood, and supported.

Navigating Conflicts and Disagreements with Empathy and Respect

Conflict is a natural and inevitable part of any relationship, but resilient relationships are characterized by the ability to navigate conflicts and disagreements with empathy and respect. This involves listening actively to the other person's perspective, seeking to understand their point of view, and finding common ground and solutions that address the needs and concerns of both parties.

To navigate conflicts and disagreements with empathy and respect, individuals should practice active listening, refraining from interrupting or dismissing the other person's feelings or opinions. Instead, they should strive to empathize with their perspective, validating their emotions and experiences, and expressing understanding and compassion.

Moreover, navigating conflicts and disagreements with empathy and respect involves communicating assertively and constructively, using "I" statements to express one's own feelings and needs without blaming or criticizing the other person. It also involves being open to feedback and compromise, and being willing to explore creative solutions that satisfy both parties.

Building Resilience Within Relationships Through Effective Communication and Conflict Resolution

Resilient relationships are built on a foundation of effective communication and conflict resolution. This involves fostering open and honest communication, expressing one's thoughts, feelings, and needs clearly and assertively, and listening actively to the other person's perspective with empathy and respect.

To build resilience within relationships through effective communication and conflict resolution, individuals should cultivate self-awareness, recognizing their own communication style and patterns, and being willing to adapt and adjust their approach to better meet the needs of the other person. They should also prioritize active listening and empathy, seeking to understand the other person's perspective and feelings before expressing their own.

Moreover, building resilience within relationships through effective communication and conflict resolution involves being proactive in addressing conflicts and disagreements as they arise, rather than allowing them to fester and escalate over time. It also involves being willing to seek outside support or guidance when needed, such as from a trusted friend, family member, or therapist, to help navigate challenging situations and find resolution.

Fostering Mutual Trust, Respect, and Understanding

At the core of resilient relationships lies mutual trust, respect, and understanding. This involves honoring each other's boundaries, values, and autonomy, and treating each other with kindness, compassion, and dignity. Fostering mutual trust, respect, and understanding requires individuals to be reliable and dependable in their actions, and to demonstrate integrity and honesty in their interactions.

To foster mutual trust, respect, and understanding within relationships, individuals should prioritize transparency and honesty, being forthcoming about their thoughts, feelings, and intentions, and avoiding deception or manipulation. They should also be consistent and reliable in their behavior, following through on their commitments and promises, and being there for each other during times of need.

Moreover, fostering mutual trust, respect, and understanding involves being willing to forgive and let go of past grievances, and to approach each other with empathy and compassion. It also involves being open to feedback and constructive criticism, and being willing to work together to address any issues or concerns that may arise.

In conclusion, resilient relationships are the bedrock of emotional well-being and fulfillment, providing comfort, support, and companionship during life's ups and downs. By cultivating strong and supportive connections with others, navigating conflicts and disagreements with empathy and respect, building resilience through effective communication and conflict resolution, and fostering mutual trust, respect, and understanding, individuals can create relationships that withstand the test of time and adversity. As Tony Robbins so aptly stated, "The quality of your life is the quality of your relationships." By investing in the quality of their relationships, individuals can enrich their lives and cultivate a sense of belonging, purpose, and fulfillment that extends far beyond themselves.

Chapter 20
Celebrating Resilience

"Resilience is the capacity to recover quickly from difficulties; toughness." - Oxford Languages

Resilience is not merely a concept but a lived experience that shapes our journey through life. It's the ability to navigate adversity, bounce back from setbacks, and emerge stronger and more resilient than before. In this chapter, we delve deeper into the importance of celebrating resilience – both in ourselves and in others. We'll explore how recognizing and celebrating resilience can serve as a powerful tool for personal growth, gratitude, and optimism as we navigate life's challenges.

Recognizing and Celebrating Resilience in Oneself and Others

The journey of resilience is marked by countless moments of courage, perseverance, and resilience. Yet, often, these moments go unnoticed or unacknowledged. Recognizing and celebrating resilience is about shining a light on these moments – both big and small – and honoring the strength and determination it takes to overcome adversity.

To recognize and celebrate resilience in oneself and others, it's essential to cultivate a mindset of appreciation and acknowledgment. This involves taking the time to reflect on past challenges and acknowledging the progress made, no matter how small. It also involves expressing gratitude for the support and encouragement received from others along the way.

Moreover, recognizing and celebrating resilience involves celebrating milestones and achievements, no matter how modest they may seem. Whether it's overcoming a fear, achieving a personal goal, or simply getting through a difficult day, every step forward is worthy of celebration. By acknowledging these moments of resilience, individuals can build confidence, self-esteem, and a sense of pride in their ability to overcome adversity.

Reflecting on Personal Growth and Accomplishments

Resilience is not just about bouncing back from adversity; it's also about growth, learning, and transformation. Reflecting on personal growth and accomplishments is an essential part of celebrating resilience, as it allows individuals to recognize how far they've come and the lessons they've learned along the way.

To reflect on personal growth and accomplishments, individuals should take time to journal, meditate, or engage in other forms of self-reflection. This involves revisiting past challenges and considering the ways in which they've shaped their character, values, and priorities. It also involves acknowledging the skills, strengths, and resources they've developed as a result of overcoming adversity.

Moreover, reflecting on personal growth and accomplishments involves celebrating progress, no matter how incremental it may be. Whether it's learning to manage stress more effectively, developing stronger relationships, or gaining a deeper understanding of oneself, every step forward is a cause for celebration. By reflecting on personal growth and accomplishments, individuals can cultivate a sense of gratitude, resilience, and optimism for the challenges that lie ahead.

Honoring the Journey of Resilience with Gratitude and Pride

The journey of resilience is not always easy, but it's a journey worth honoring and celebrating. Honoring the journey of resilience with gratitude and pride is about recognizing the strength, courage, and perseverance it takes to overcome adversity and thrive in the face of challenges.

To honor the journey of resilience with gratitude and pride, individuals should take time to express appreciation for the lessons learned and the growth experienced along the way. This involves acknowledging the people, experiences, and opportunities that have supported and guided them on their journey of resilience. It also involves expressing gratitude for the strength and resilience that resides within them, enabling them to overcome even the toughest of obstacles.

Moreover, honoring the journey of resilience with gratitude and pride involves celebrating one's resilience story as a source of inspiration and empowerment for others. By sharing their experiences and insights, individuals can offer hope, encouragement, and support to those who may be facing similar challenges. It's about recognizing that resilience is not just a personal attribute but a shared human experience that connects us all.

Looking Forward with Optimism and Resilience for the Challenges Ahead

Celebrating resilience is not just about looking back on past accomplishments; it's also about looking forward with optimism and resilience for the challenges that lie ahead. It's about recognizing that resilience is not a destination but a journey – one that continues to unfold and evolve with each new experience.

Looking forward with optimism and resilience for the challenges ahead involves cultivating a mindset of possibility and growth. It's about approaching challenges with curiosity, openness, and a willingness to learn and adapt. It's also about embracing uncertainty and change as opportunities for growth and transformation.

Moreover, looking forward with optimism and resilience for the challenges ahead involves setting goals and intentions that reflect one's values, passions, and aspirations. It's about channeling one's resilience into purposeful action, making a positive impact in the world and leaving a legacy of resilience for future generations to come.

In conclusion, celebrating resilience is about honoring the journey of growth, courage, and transformation that unfolds in the face of adversity. By recognizing and celebrating resilience in oneself and others, reflecting on personal growth and accomplishments, honoring the journey of resilience with gratitude and pride, and looking forward with optimism and resilience for the challenges ahead, individuals can cultivate a sense of empowerment, purpose, and resilience that propels them towards a brighter and more resilient future. As we celebrate resilience, we honor the human spirit's capacity to endure, adapt, and thrive – no matter what challenges may come our way.

Chapter 21
Cultivating Resilient Mindsets

"Our greatest glory is not in never falling, but in rising every time we fall." - Confucius

Resilience isn't just about bouncing back from adversity; it's about how we perceive and respond to challenges. In this chapter, we delve into the importance of cultivating resilient mindsets – the mental attitudes and perspectives that enable us to face adversity with courage, optimism, and perseverance. We'll explore how embracing a growth mindset, harnessing the power of reframing and resilience-building techniques, and recognizing the role of mindset in shaping resilience and renewal can empower us to overcome obstacles and thrive in the face of adversity.

Embracing a Growth Mindset in the Face of Challenges

At the heart of resilient mindsets lies a growth mindset – the belief that our abilities and intelligence can be developed through dedication and hard work. Instead of viewing challenges as insurmountable obstacles, individuals with a growth mindset see them as opportunities for learning, growth, and self-improvement.

Embracing a growth mindset in the face of challenges involves reframing setbacks as learning experiences, rather than failures. It's about approaching challenges with curiosity, openness, and a willingness to experiment and learn from mistakes. It's also about believing in one's ability to overcome obstacles through effort, persistence, and resilience.

To cultivate a growth mindset, individuals should practice self-awareness and self-reflection, challenging limiting beliefs and replacing them with empowering and optimistic thoughts. They should also seek out feedback and constructive criticism, viewing it as an opportunity for growth and development. By embracing a growth mindset, individuals can unlock their full potential and navigate challenges with confidence and resilience.

Cultivating Resilience Through Optimism and Perseverance

Optimism and perseverance are essential components of resilient mindsets, enabling individuals to maintain a positive outlook and stay motivated in the face of adversity. Optimism involves maintaining a hopeful and positive attitude, even in the face of setbacks and challenges. Perseverance involves staying committed and determined to achieve one's goals, despite obstacles and setbacks along the way.

Cultivating resilience through optimism and perseverance involves reframing negative thoughts and beliefs into more positive and empowering ones. It's about focusing on solutions rather than dwelling on problems, and maintaining a sense of hope and optimism, even in the face of uncertainty.

Moreover, cultivating resilience through optimism and perseverance involves setting realistic goals and taking proactive steps towards achieving them, despite obstacles and setbacks. It's about staying focused and motivated, even when the going gets tough, and persevering in the pursuit of one's dreams and aspirations.

Harnessing the Power of Reframing and Resilience-Building Techniques

Reframing is a powerful resilience-building technique that involves changing the way we perceive and interpret adversity. Instead of viewing challenges as threats, individuals can reframe them as opportunities for growth, learning, and self-discovery. Reframing involves shifting our perspective, focusing on the positive aspects of a situation, and finding meaning and purpose in adversity.

There are several resilience-building techniques that individuals can use to harness the power of reframing and cultivate resilient mindsets. These techniques include cognitive restructuring, which involves identifying and challenging negative thought patterns and replacing them with more positive and empowering ones. They also include gratitude practices, mindfulness meditation, and visualization exercises, which can help individuals cultivate a sense of optimism, resilience, and inner strength.

By harnessing the power of reframing and resilience-building techniques, individuals can cultivate resilient mindsets that enable them to face adversity with courage, optimism, and perseverance. They can develop the mental attitudes and perspectives that empower them to overcome obstacles and thrive in the face of challenges.

Recognizing the Role of Mindset in Shaping Resilience and Renewal

Mindset plays a crucial role in shaping resilience and renewal, influencing how we perceive and respond to challenges. Individuals with resilient mindsets are better able to cope with stress, bounce back from setbacks, and adapt to change. They approach challenges with a sense of optimism, viewing them as opportunities for growth and self-improvement.

Recognizing the role of mindset in shaping resilience and renewal involves cultivating self-awareness and mindfulness, observing and understanding the thoughts, beliefs, and attitudes that influence our behavior and emotions. It also involves practicing self-compassion and acceptance, acknowledging our strengths and limitations, and treating ourselves with kindness and understanding.

Moreover, recognizing the role of mindset in shaping resilience and renewal involves taking proactive steps to cultivate a resilient mindset, such as practicing gratitude, optimism, and perseverance. By embracing a growth mindset, harnessing the power of reframing and resilience-building techniques, and recognizing the role of mindset in shaping resilience and renewal, individuals can cultivate the mental attitudes and perspectives that empower them to overcome obstacles and thrive in the face of adversity.

In conclusion, cultivating resilient mindsets is essential for navigating life's challenges with courage, optimism, and perseverance. By embracing a growth mindset, harnessing the power of reframing and resilience-building techniques, and recognizing the role of mindset in shaping resilience and renewal, individuals can develop the mental attitudes and perspectives that empower them to overcome obstacles and thrive in the face of adversity. As Confucius so aptly stated, "Our greatest glory is not in never falling, but in rising every time we fall." By cultivating resilient mindsets, individuals can rise stronger and more resilient than ever before, ready to face whatever challenges may come their way.

Chapter 22

Building Resilient Communities

"Alone we can do so little; together we can do so much." - Helen Keller

In the face of adversity, resilient communities stand as pillars of support, solidarity, and strength. This chapter explores the vital importance of building resilient communities - spaces where individuals come together to foster connection, support, and empowerment. We'll delve into the principles and practices that underpin resilient communities, from fostering connection and support to empowering individuals to contribute to collective resilience, creating inclusive spaces that foster belonging and solidarity, and mobilizing resources and networks to address shared challenges.

Fostering Connection and Support Within Communities

At the heart of resilient communities lies a sense of connection and support - the understanding that we are all in this together and that we can rely on one another for help, comfort, and encouragement. Fostering connection and support within communities involves creating spaces where individuals feel welcomed, valued, and understood, and where they can come together to share their experiences, challenges, and triumphs.

To foster connection and support within communities, it's essential to prioritize communication, collaboration, and cooperation. This involves creating opportunities for individuals to come together, whether in person or virtually, to engage in meaningful conversations, activities, and initiatives that promote connection and belonging. It also involves fostering a culture of empathy, compassion, and solidarity, where

135

individuals feel safe and supported in sharing their thoughts, feelings, and experiences with others.

Moreover, fostering connection and support within communities involves recognizing and addressing the unique needs and challenges faced by different individuals and groups. It's about creating inclusive spaces that celebrate diversity, equity, and inclusion and that honor the voices and experiences of all community members. By fostering connection and support within communities, we can build strong, resilient networks of support that enable individuals to thrive and succeed, even in the face of adversity.

Empowering Individuals to Contribute to Collective Resilience

Resilient communities empower individuals to contribute to collective resilience – to be active participants in shaping the future of their communities and addressing shared challenges together. Empowering individuals to contribute to collective resilience involves providing opportunities for leadership, collaboration, and civic engagement, where individuals can make meaningful contributions to the well-being and prosperity of their communities.

To empower individuals to contribute to collective resilience, it's essential to foster a sense of agency, autonomy, and ownership. This involves encouraging individuals to identify and pursue opportunities for leadership and participation, whether through volunteering, advocacy, or community organizing. It also involves providing resources, support, and training to help individuals develop the skills, confidence, and resilience needed to make a positive impact in their communities.

Moreover, empowering individuals to contribute to collective resilience involves recognizing and valuing the unique talents, strengths, and perspectives that each individual brings to the table. It's about creating opportunities for collaboration and cooperation, where individuals can work together towards common goals and aspirations. By empowering individuals to contribute to collective resilience, we can harness the collective wisdom, creativity, and energy of our communities to address shared challenges and build a brighter, more resilient future for all.

Creating Inclusive Spaces That Foster Belonging and Solidarity

Resilient communities are built on a foundation of inclusivity, where every individual feels a sense of belonging, acceptance, and solidarity. Creating inclusive spaces that foster belonging and solidarity involves recognizing and addressing the barriers and disparities that prevent certain individuals and groups from fully participating and thriving in their communities.

To create inclusive spaces that foster belonging and solidarity, it's essential to prioritize diversity, equity, and inclusion in all aspects of community life. This involves actively seeking out and amplifying the voices and experiences of marginalized and underrepresented individuals and groups, and ensuring that their needs and perspectives are heard, valued, and respected.

Moreover, creating inclusive spaces that foster belonging and solidarity involves challenging stereotypes, biases, and discrimination, and promoting a culture of empathy, understanding, and mutual respect. It's about creating opportunities for dialogue, education, and awareness-building, where individuals can learn from one another and work together to create a more just, equitable, and inclusive society.

Mobilizing Resources and Networks to Address Shared Challenges

Resilient communities are proactive and resourceful, mobilizing their collective resources and networks to address shared challenges and opportunities. Mobilizing resources and networks to address shared challenges involves leveraging the strengths, assets, and connections of community members to develop innovative solutions and initiatives that promote resilience and well-being.

To mobilize resources and networks to address shared challenges, it's essential to foster collaboration and cooperation among community members, organizations, and institutions. This involves building partnerships and alliances that bring together diverse perspectives, expertise, and resources to address complex issues and achieve common goals.

Moreover, mobilizing resources and networks to address shared challenges involves empowering individuals and groups to take collective action and make a positive impact in their communities. It's about providing support, training, and guidance to help community members develop the skills, confidence, and resilience needed to advocate for change and mobilize support for important causes.

In conclusion, building resilient communities is essential for creating a more just, equitable, and sustainable world. By fostering connection and support, empowering individuals to contribute to collective resilience, creating inclusive spaces that foster belonging and solidarity, and mobilizing resources and networks to address shared challenges, we can create communities that are strong, resilient, and vibrant – places where every individual has the opportunity to thrive and succeed, no matter what challenges may come their way. As Helen Keller so eloquently stated, "Alone we can do so little; together we can do so much." By working together, we can build communities that are resilient, inclusive, and empowered to create positive change in the world.

Chapter 23

Sustaining Resilient Practices

"The secret of change is to focus all of your energy, not on fighting the old, but on building the new." - Socrates

Resilience isn't just about weathering the storm; it's about building structures and practices that allow us to thrive in the face of adversity. In this chapter, we'll explore the importance of sustaining resilient practices – the rituals, routines, and habits that promote resilience and renewal in our lives. From establishing rituals and routines to integrating resilience-building practices into daily life, monitoring progress, and nurturing a sustainable approach to resilience and renewal, we'll uncover the key principles and strategies for maintaining resilience in the long term.

Establishing Rituals and Routines that Promote Resilience

Rituals and routines provide structure and stability in our lives, anchoring us during times of uncertainty and upheaval. Establishing rituals and routines that promote resilience involves identifying practices that nourish and replenish us – physically, mentally, emotionally, and spiritually – and integrating them into our daily lives.

To establish rituals and routines that promote resilience, it's essential to prioritize self-care, wellness, and well-being. This may involve setting aside time each day for activities such as meditation, exercise, journaling, or spending time in nature – practices that replenish our energy and restore our sense of balance and harmony.

Moreover, establishing rituals and routines that promote resilience involves creating consistency and predictability in our daily lives. This may involve establishing morning and evening routines, setting boundaries around work and technology, and creating rituals that mark transitions between different activities and roles.

By establishing rituals and routines that promote resilience, we can create a foundation of stability and support that sustains us through life's challenges and uncertainties.

Integrating Resilience-Building Practices into Daily Life

Resilience-building practices are most effective when they become an integral part of our daily lives – woven into the fabric of our routines and habits. Integrating resilience-building practices into daily life involves identifying small, manageable actions that promote resilience and well-being and incorporating them into our daily routines and activities.

To integrate resilience-building practices into daily life, it's essential to start small and focus on consistency and sustainability. This may involve setting achievable goals and gradually increasing the intensity or duration of resilience-building activities over time. It's also important to be flexible and adaptive, adjusting our practices and routines as needed to accommodate changes in our circumstances and priorities.

Moreover, integrating resilience-building practices into daily life involves cultivating mindfulness and presence, bringing our full attention and awareness to each moment and experience. This may involve practicing mindfulness meditation, deep breathing exercises, or other mindfulness techniques that help us stay grounded and centered amidst the busyness and distractions of daily life.

By integrating resilience-building practices into daily life, we can cultivate a strong foundation of resilience that sustains us through life's ups and downs.

Monitoring Progress and Adjusting Strategies as Needed

Sustaining resilient practices requires ongoing attention and effort, as well as a willingness to monitor our progress and adjust our strategies as needed. Monitoring progress and adjusting strategies involves regularly reflecting on our resilience-building efforts, assessing what's working well and what could be improved, and making adjustments accordingly.

To monitor progress and adjust strategies as needed, it's essential to cultivate self-awareness and reflection, paying attention to our thoughts, feelings, and behaviors and their impact on our resilience and well-being. This may involve keeping a journal, tracking our resilience-building activities, and seeking feedback from trusted friends, family members, or mentors.

Moreover, monitoring progress and adjusting strategies as needed involves being adaptable and flexible, willing to experiment with new approaches and learn from our experiences. It's important to recognize that resilience is not a one-size-fits-all endeavor and that what works well for one person may not work as well for another. By staying open to new ideas and approaches, we can continue to refine and optimize our resilience-building efforts over time.

By monitoring progress and adjusting strategies as needed, we can ensure that our resilience-building practices remain effective and sustainable in the long term.

Nurturing a Sustainable Approach to Resilience and Renewal

Ultimately, sustaining resilient practices requires nurturing a sustainable approach to resilience and renewal – one that prioritizes balance, self-care, and holistic well-being. Nurturing a sustainable approach to resilience and renewal involves recognizing that resilience is not just about bouncing back from adversity but about fostering growth, learning, and self-discovery.

To nurture a sustainable approach to resilience and renewal, it's essential to prioritize self-care and well-being, making time for activities that nourish and replenish us – physically, mentally, emotionally, and spiritually. This may involve setting boundaries around work and technology, prioritizing rest and relaxation, and engaging in activities that bring us joy and fulfillment.

Moreover, nurturing a sustainable approach to resilience and renewal involves cultivating a sense of purpose and meaning in our lives, connecting with our values, passions, and aspirations, and aligning our actions with what truly matters to us. It's about recognizing that resilience is not just about surviving; it's about thriving – living a life that is rich, meaningful, and fulfilling.

By nurturing a sustainable approach to resilience and renewal, we can create a life that is characterized by vitality, purpose, and resilience – one that enables us to navigate life's challenges with courage, grace, and optimism.

In conclusion, sustaining resilient practices requires intention, effort, and a commitment to ongoing growth and learning. By establishing rituals and routines that promote resilience, integrating resilience-building practices into daily life, monitoring progress and adjusting strategies as needed, and nurturing a sustainable approach to resilience and renewal, we can cultivate a strong foundation of resilience that sustains us through life's challenges and enables us to thrive in the face of adversity. As Socrates so wisely stated, "The secret of change is to focus all of your energy, not on fighting the old, but on building the new." By focusing our energy on building resilient practices and habits, we can create a brighter, more resilient future for ourselves and those around us.

Chapter 24

Resilience in Times of Crisis

"In the midst of chaos, there is also opportunity." - Sun Tzu

Crises are inevitable in life, but how we respond to them can make all the difference. This chapter delves into the crucial topic of resilience in times of crisis – how individuals and organizations can effectively navigate challenges, adapt to change, and emerge stronger and more resilient than before. We'll explore the principles and strategies for responding effectively to crisis situations with resilience, developing crisis management skills and strategies, leveraging adversity as a catalyst for innovation and growth, and building organizational resilience to withstand and thrive during crises.

Responding Effectively to Crisis Situations with Resilience

In times of crisis, resilience is more important than ever. Responding effectively to crisis situations with resilience involves maintaining composure, clarity, and adaptability in the face of adversity. It's about staying grounded, resourceful, and focused on finding solutions, even amidst chaos and uncertainty.

To respond effectively to crisis situations with resilience, it's essential to prioritize preparation, planning, and readiness. This involves anticipating potential crises, identifying risks and vulnerabilities, and developing robust contingency plans and protocols to mitigate and manage them effectively. It also involves fostering a culture of resilience within organizations, where individuals are empowered to take proactive action and collaborate effectively in response to crises.

Moreover, responding effectively to crisis situations

with resilience involves maintaining open lines of communication, both internally and externally, and providing timely and accurate information to stakeholders. It's about building trust, transparency, and confidence in the organization's ability to navigate challenges and emerge stronger on the other side.

By responding effectively to crisis situations with resilience, individuals and organizations can minimize the impact of crises, preserve essential functions and services, and position themselves for recovery and renewal.

Developing Crisis Management Skills and Strategies

Crisis management is a critical skill set for individuals and organizations alike, enabling them to effectively identify, assess, and respond to crises in a timely and coordinated manner. Developing crisis management skills and strategies involves building a comprehensive understanding of crisis dynamics, as well as the tools, techniques, and best practices for managing them effectively.

To develop crisis management skills and strategies, it's essential to invest in training, education, and professional development. This may involve participating in crisis simulation exercises, attending workshops and seminars, or pursuing certifications in crisis management and emergency preparedness. It's also important to stay informed about emerging trends and developments in crisis management, including new technologies, methodologies, and approaches.

Moreover, developing crisis management skills and strategies involves cultivating a proactive and forward-thinking mindset, where individuals and organizations are constantly scanning the horizon for potential threats and opportunities. It's about being agile, adaptive, and responsive in the face of change, and leveraging lessons learned from past crises to inform future decision-making and planning.

By developing crisis management skills and strategies, individuals and organizations can enhance their ability to anticipate, prepare for, and respond to crises effectively, minimizing disruptions and maximizing resilience.

Leveraging Adversity as a Catalyst for Innovation and Growth

While crises are often seen as obstacles to be overcome, they can also be opportunities for innovation, growth, and transformation. Leveraging adversity as a catalyst for innovation and growth involves reframing challenges as opportunities for learning, creativity, and innovation. It's about embracing change, uncertainty, and disruption as catalysts for positive change and renewal.

To leverage adversity as a catalyst for innovation and growth, it's essential to foster a culture of experimentation, creativity, and resilience within organizations. This involves encouraging individuals to think outside the box, take calculated risks, and explore new ideas and approaches to problem-solving. It also involves providing support, resources, and incentives to encourage innovation and experimentation, and celebrating successes and failures alike as opportunities for learning and growth.

Moreover, leveraging adversity as a catalyst for innovation and growth involves cultivating a mindset of resilience and optimism, where individuals are empowered to see challenges as opportunities for growth and development. It's about reframing setbacks as stepping stones to success, and using adversity as a springboard for personal and organizational transformation.

By leveraging adversity as a catalyst for innovation and growth, individuals and organizations can turn crises into opportunities, emerging stronger, more agile, and more resilient than before.

Building Organizational Resilience to Withstand and Thrive During Crises

Organizational resilience is essential for navigating crises effectively, enabling organizations to withstand shocks, adapt to change, and emerge stronger and more resilient than before. Building organizational resilience involves creating structures, systems, and cultures that support adaptability, flexibility, and innovation, even in the face of adversity.

To build organizational resilience, it's essential to prioritize leadership, communication, and collaboration. This involves fostering a culture of trust, transparency, and accountability, where leaders are accessible, responsive, and supportive, and where employees feel empowered to contribute their ideas and insights. It also involves investing in robust communication networks and channels, both internally and externally, to ensure that information flows freely and accurately throughout the organization.

Moreover, building organizational resilience involves diversifying and strengthening organizational capabilities and resources, including human, financial, technological, and physical assets. This may involve developing cross-functional teams, building strategic partnerships and alliances, and investing in technology and infrastructure that enhance agility and adaptability.

By building organizational resilience, organizations can weather crises more effectively, minimize disruptions to operations and services, and position themselves for long-term success and sustainability.

In conclusion, resilience in times of crisis is not just about surviving; it's about thriving – emerging stronger, more agile, and more resilient than before. By responding effectively to crisis situations with resilience, developing crisis management skills and strategies, leveraging adversity as a catalyst for innovation and growth, and building organizational resilience to withstand and thrive during crises, individuals and organizations can navigate challenges with confidence, courage, and optimism. As Sun Tzu so wisely stated, "In the midst of chaos, there is also opportunity." By embracing adversity as an opportunity for growth and transformation, we can emerge stronger and more resilient on the other side, ready to face whatever challenges may come our way.

Chapter 25
Legacy of Resilience

"The future belongs to those who believe in the beauty of their dreams." - Eleanor Roosevelt

Resilience isn't just about overcoming challenges in the present – it's also about leaving a lasting legacy that inspires and empowers future generations. This chapter explores the profound impact of resilience on personal and collective legacies, the importance of passing down resilience skills and values to future generations, celebrating the resilience of ancestors and historical figures, and inspiring hope and courage for a resilient future.

Reflecting on the Impact of Resilience on Personal and Collective Legacies

The legacy of resilience extends far beyond individual experiences, shaping the course of families, communities, and societies for generations to come. Reflecting on the impact of resilience on personal and collective legacies involves recognizing the profound influence that resilient individuals and communities have on shaping the world around them.

Resilience leaves an indelible mark on personal legacies, shaping the values, beliefs, and character of individuals and their descendants. It's about passing down stories of triumph over adversity, perseverance in the face of challenges, and resilience in the pursuit of dreams. These stories serve as a source of inspiration and strength, reminding future generations of their capacity to overcome obstacles and achieve greatness.

Moreover, resilience shapes collective legacies, influencing the culture, identity, and trajectory of communities and societies. It's about recognizing the resilience of communities that have endured hardship and adversity, and celebrating their resilience as a testament to the human spirit. These collective legacies of resilience inspire solidarity, compassion, and social change, shaping a brighter, more resilient future for all.

Passing Down Resilience Skills and Values to Future Generations

Passing down resilience skills and values to future generations is essential for ensuring that the legacy of resilience endures. It's about equipping young people with the tools, knowledge, and mindset they need to navigate life's challenges with courage, strength, and grace.

To pass down resilience skills and values to future generations, it's essential to lead by example, modeling resilience in action and demonstrating the importance of perseverance, optimism, and adaptability. It's also about creating opportunities for young people to develop resilience through experiences that challenge and empower them, whether through outdoor adventures, volunteer work, or creative pursuits.

Moreover, passing down resilience skills and values to future generations involves fostering open and honest communication, providing a safe space for young people to express their thoughts, feelings, and concerns, and offering support and guidance as they navigate life's ups and downs. It's about instilling in them a sense of self-belief, resilience, and agency, empowering them to face adversity with confidence and resilience.

Celebrating the Resilience of Ancestors and Historical Figures

The resilience of ancestors and historical figures serves as a beacon of hope and inspiration, reminding us of the power of the human spirit to triumph over adversity. Celebrating their resilience honors their legacy and reinforces the values and principles that they stood for.

To celebrate the resilience of ancestors and historical figures, it's essential to preserve and share their stories, highlighting the challenges they faced and the courage and resilience they demonstrated in overcoming them. It's also about recognizing the impact of their resilience on shaping the course of history, inspiring generations to come with their acts of bravery, compassion, and resilience.

Moreover, celebrating the resilience of ancestors and historical figures involves honoring their contributions to society, whether through monuments, memorials, or commemorative events that recognize their achievements and sacrifices. It's about ensuring that their legacy lives on, inspiring future generations to continue their work and carry forward their values and ideals.

Inspiring Hope and Courage for a Resilient Future

As we reflect on the legacy of resilience, we must also look to the future with hope and courage, knowing that we have the power to shape a more resilient world for generations to come. Inspiring hope and courage for a resilient future involves cultivating a sense of optimism, possibility, and agency, empowering individuals and communities to create positive change in the world.

To inspire hope and courage for a resilient future, it's essential to foster a culture of resilience and innovation, where individuals are encouraged to dream big, think creatively, and take bold action in pursuit of their goals. It's also about fostering connections and collaboration, bringing together diverse perspectives, talents, and resources to address shared challenges and create a more resilient and sustainable world.

Moreover, inspiring hope and courage for a resilient future involves nurturing a sense of responsibility and stewardship for future generations, recognizing the interconnectedness of all life and the importance of preserving and protecting the planet for generations to come. It's about instilling in individuals and communities a sense of purpose and meaning, empowering them to make a positive impact in the world and leave behind a legacy of resilience and hope for future generations.

In conclusion, the legacy of resilience is a testament to the power of the human spirit to overcome adversity, create positive change, and shape a better world for generations to come. By reflecting on the impact of resilience on personal and collective legacies, passing down resilience skills and values to future generations, celebrating the resilience of ancestors and historical figures, and inspiring hope and courage for a resilient future, we can ensure that the legacy of resilience endures, empowering individuals and communities to thrive in the face of whatever challenges may come their way. As Eleanor Roosevelt so wisely stated, "The future belongs to those who believe in the beauty of their dreams." By believing in the beauty of our dreams and embracing the resilience within us, we can create a brighter, more resilient future for all.

CONCLUSION

As we come to the end of our journey, let us take a moment to reflect on all that we have learned and experienced together. We have explored the depths of resilience and renewal, delving into the strategies, insights, and wisdom that empower us to navigate life's challenges with courage, grace, and inner strength. Along the way, we have encountered stories of triumph over adversity, practical strategies for building resilience, and timeless principles for thriving in turbulent times.

Through our exploration, we have come to understand that resilience is not just about bouncing back from setbacks; it's about embracing change, finding meaning in adversity, and harnessing the power of our inner resources to create positive change in the world. It's about recognizing that challenges are not obstacles to be overcome but opportunities for growth and transformation. It's about cultivating a mindset of resilience, where every setback is seen as a stepping stone to success, and every failure is viewed as a lesson in disguise.

As we look to the future, let us carry forward the lessons we have learned and the insights we have gained on our journey. Let us embrace the challenges that lie ahead with courage, optimism, and resilience, knowing that we have the strength and fortitude to overcome whatever obstacles may come our way. Let us pass down the legacy of resilience to future generations, inspiring hope and courage for a brighter, more resilient future for all.

In closing, I would like to express my deepest gratitude to you, the reader, for joining me on this journey of exploration and discovery. May the insights and wisdom shared in these pages serve as a source of inspiration and guidance as you navigate life's challenges with grace, courage, and inner strength. And may you continue to thrive in turbulent times, embracing change, finding meaning in adversity, and harnessing the power of resilience to create a life of purpose, fulfillment, and joy.

ABOUT THE AUTHOR

Adeel Anjum is a visionary business leader with an illustrious career spanning over 20 years in strategic management and consulting. With a dynamic background that includes diverse industries such as sports retail, fashion retail, food retail, oil & gas, F&B, fitness & leisure, as well as technology & telecom retail, Adeel has amassed a wealth of experience and expertise in driving organizational success.

As a thought leader, Adeel Anjum stands at the forefront of shaping the business community through his pioneering work, insightful writings, and groundbreaking research. With a commitment to innovation and a deep understanding of Industry dynamics, Adeel Anjum inspires and guides fellow professionals, fostering a culture of continuous learning and strategic evolution within the business landscape.

Driven by a steadfast commitment to contribute to the business world, I am channeling my knowledge and experience into meaningful narratives within my books. My aim is to offer valuable insights, lessons, and strategies that empower individuals and organizations. Through the written word, I aspire to give back to the business community, sharing the wisdom gained on my journey and inspiring others to achieve their fullest potential and mindfulness.

Made in United States
Orlando, FL
05 May 2024